GOD'S KITCHEN

*Mike Bull is a graphic designer who lives and works
in the Blue Mountains west of Sydney, Australia.
His passion is understanding and teaching the Bible.*

Also by this author:

Totus Christus: A Biblical Theology
of the Whole Christ

Bible Matrix: An Introduction
to the DNA of the Scriptures

Bible Matrix II: The Covenant Key

GOD'S KITCHEN

Theology you can eat & drink

WestBow Press books may be ordered through booksellers or by contacting:

WestBow Press
A Division of Thomas Nelson
1663 Liberty Drive
Bloomington, IN 47403
www.westbowpress.com
1-(866) 928-1240

ISBN: 978-1-44-977940-5 (sc)
ISBN: 978-1-44-977941-2 (e)
Library of Congress Control Number: 2012924142

Designed and typeset by Michael Bull

Printed in the United States of America

WestBow Press rev. date: 1/24/2013

WESTBOW
PRESS
A DIVISION OF THOMAS NELSON

In memory of my mother, Helen,
who fed us too well
and taught us how to laugh till we cried.

Thanks to my friends David Deutsch,
Albert Garlando, Jared Leonard,
Steven Opp and Andrew Welch
for their invaluable help in the kitchen.

Menu

Saved by fire...

The God of the Old Testament is a butcher only because the Christ of the New Testament is a chef.

The best cuts

INGREDIENTS & METHOD

THE BIBLE IS A VIOLENT, BLOODY BOOK, and modern Christians have a problem with that. Atheists are right to accuse us of being embarrassed by our own scriptures.

Although desensitized by the media to violence and bloodshed in the abstract, in reality, modern Westerners are averse to the sight of blood. Some Christians even shy from its mere mention. After two world wars, this is perhaps understandable. War is no longer considered to be glorious. Yet we enjoy the freedoms that were won, for blood is not only a reminder of death; it is also the messenger, the *mediator,* of new life.

Not only is the Bible a bloody book, it is "unscientific" and therefore an irrational vestige of an intolerant and inequitable religion as far as modern society is concerned.

Without the Old Testament, however, it is impossible to interpret the world rightly. Science cuts things up and tells us what they are made of, but its scope is limited when it comes to telling us what they are actually for.

Modern theologians are not much better when it comes to the "world" of the Bible. The constraint of their scientistic[1] mindset leaves them struggling, clueless, with what the Apostle Paul means by the term "flesh," and yet also struggling with the significance of the careful instructions for the head, skin, flesh, offal, fat and legs of the sacrificial animals in Leviticus. The relevance of the fact that these fleshly animals were blameless substitutes for sinful, fleshly men entirely escapes them. Darwinism didn't only rewrite history; it usurped the intended, holy purpose of homology.[2]

The emaciated theology that remains to us is divorced from the real world. Peter Leithart writes:

> Theology is a "Victorian" enterprise, neoclassically bright and neat and clean, nothing out of place. Whereas the Bible talks about hair, blood, sweat, entrails, menstruation and genital emissions...
>
> Ponder these questions: Do theologians talk about the world the same way the Bible does? Do theologians talk about the same *world* the Bible does?[3]

---

1 Scientism is the belief that the investigative methods of the physical sciences are applicable to all fields of inquiry.
2 In biology, homology is the comparison of similar organs in different species. Darwinism asserts that these are evidence of common ancestry rather than a common Designer. Recent discoveries have largely negated homology as proof of evolution. Despite this, homology is still presented as a major proof of the theory.
3 Peter J. Leithart, *Against Christianity*, p. 47.

And yet, ironically, this divorce *directly affects* the real world. *Cultus* inevitably informs culture. Many Westerners anxiously strip the bloody flesh from their menus precisely because we Christians have stripped it from our religion.

Even the meatiest Christians, the respectable evangelicals, present a Christianity that is far cleaner and far leaner than the bloody history in the Book they claim to represent. They have developed a taste for cold, waxen theologies entirely distracted from the flesh-and-blood world of the Bible. They spend their time squabbling over the nuances of their own abstract definitions of isolated crumbs. They traffic in thickening agents and food extenders and package their pasty, bloated tomes for sale as royal feasts for the starving soul.

Certainly, there is some meat to be thankful for, but modern congregations prefer their theology to be served precut, pre-marinated and even pre-digested where possible. It appears as if by magic in tidy cling-wrapped trays or microwaveable bags.

Our hearts desire—and *require*—meat, but we moderns are too squeamish to be concerned with the "primitive" processes of God. We are too busy, or too lazy, to cut and chew, and we wonder why our Gospel seems to have lost its teeth. Why is so much preaching so bad? Because only a blameless, bloodied, sacrificial lamb is worthy to open the scroll.

Just as urban school children take excursions to farms to discover the origins of the food in the supermarket, so modern Christians urgently need a raw experience of the Old Testament to truly understand the Gospel of Christ.

The need of the hour is a fresh return to interpreting the world in the light of the Scriptures. Real theology deals with the physical, with milk and honey, flesh and blood, bread, oil and wine. It is nourishment for children, wisdom for kings, and courage for prophets.

Throughout history, the Word of God has been given to build the Church. As with our own fleshly bodies, we need not be ashamed of anything in the Bible. As with the Body of Christ, every part of it has a holy purpose.

INGREDIENTS

This little book is spiritual meat, and it begins where all meat does: not at the dinner table, not in the kitchen, nor even at the market. It begins in the *abattoir*.

Its roots go back even further than the slaughterhouse to a very fruitful field. The ruminations of James Jordan, Peter Leithart and Douglas Wilson have cured me of the gnosticism I inherited from my culture, and given me a deeper appreciation of the Scriptures, the natural world, the activities of human life, and the salient Words built into every created thing.

Many of the following chapters are based particularly

on Jordan's exposition of the Communion rite as a process of maturity. More generally, his approach to the Scriptures is helpful in gaining a biblical worldview. The Bible is its own "environment" and speaks its own "language." It took me some time to get used to the gutsy way in which Jordan thinks, yet his hermeneutic is not new; it was the way most people thought before the modern era. Neither is this symbolic method of thinking dead. It is precisely the means that poets, novelists and screenwriters have employed to captivate our imaginations throughout history. The problem with almost all Western theology is, quite simply, a complete lack of imagination that results in a sort of "misclassification" of the Scriptures. We force the Bible into our own molds, instead of letting it mold us.

Having glutted myself on Jordan, Leithart and Wilson, the following work may be less of a dish prepared from their raw materials than it is simply playing with my food. Or perhaps the discipline of writing has presented a means of chewing it up, of working out its implications. Whatever its faults, this material is served in the hope that it will further feed the biblical imagination.

While I believe there is enough here to delight both the inexperienced and the jaded palates, some of the following "cuts" might appear unpalatable, or even indigestible. If some connection is assumed that you struggle to see, make a note of it, but keep reading. Like a novel or a movie, this book requires some faith in the author, that the things which don't make sense at first reading actually do make sense in the big picture as part of the writer's "world." As one becomes familiar with this world, the details eventually fall into place. The bonus here is that the world which I hope is slowly becoming second nature to you is not only the world of the Bible, it is a revelation of the true, but unfamiliar, nature of the world in which we actually live.[4]

None of the following articles is raw, but some might be half-baked, and other offerings may be overdone, however, God loves a messy kitchen. He withholds many certainties from us for good reason. We are called to unearth and to experiment with what He has provided; to discover (within biblical bounds) new tastes and novel combinations appropriate to the needs of the hour; to develop a mature sense (as His royal cupbearers) that discerns between good and evil; and, most importantly of all, to present or *serve* the results of our faithful labors at the Table of the Nations. Explorative theology is a form of gratitude to the Father, whom it pleased to give us freely His only Son as Bread and Wine, stature and wisdom, the foundation and celebration of all abundant living.

---

4 On page 334 there is a list of other books that will help you to gain a truly biblical worldview.

METHOD

In one way or another, all of the following essays are written in blood. Each is a variation on the fundamental theme of the Bible, which is the movement from *Creation* to *Glorification*. God speaks something (or someone) into being, sets it apart, cuts it up, and makes something (or someone) new out of it. We see this in the Creation Week, in the construction of Eve, in the building of the nation of Israel, in the Eucharist, in the death and resurrection of Christ, and of course, in the shape of the entire Bible. I call this the "Bible Matrix." Of necessity, this book contains occasional references to this structure because it is the way God does everything He does. For those who are unfamiliar with it, I have included some "kitchen utensils" at the end of this introduction. If further study interests you, seek out my other books on this fascinating subject.

Perhaps more relevant is the fact that we see this same pattern in the process of sacrifice. God gave us food to teach us about life and death. God gave us sacrifice to teach us about death and resurrection. Jordan observes that the Ascension Offering in Leviticus 1 is a recapitulation of the Creation Week, but carried out in flesh and blood. Through the microcosmic world of Israel's priesthood and Tabernacle, God was indeed already making all things new. It was "liturgical surgery." The history of God's people is preparation for a macrocosmic feast.

Every constructive process carried out by Man follows a similar pattern to that laid down by the Creator. This means that focusing on food as a foundation for biblical studies is not a perverse idea. The history of Man begins with two fruit trees, and a single commandment pertaining to food. We prepare food for *our*selves as God prepares us for *Him*self. This book is not so much about food as it is about *us* as holy sacrificial food. The art of cooking is close to the heart of the God who is a consuming fire. At the very least, I hope this little book gives you a greater appetite for God, the original and final host.

So, take a seat. Peruse the menu. The food here is unusual, and the chef is moody, but no one ever leaves without having tried something new.

The drinks waiter will be with you directly.

I didn't need these things
I didn't need them, oh
Pointless artifacts
From a mediocre past
So I shed my clothes, I shed my flesh
Down to the bone and burned the rest

—Frightened Rabbit, *Things.*

The knife drawer

The necessary practice of theology is the Spirit's invitation to the Church to "divide up" and take an increasing possession of the Bible. The very mind of God is part of our glorious inheritance.

Creation

Creation - **Day 1:**
Light - Night and Day

Division - **Day 2:**
Waters - Above and Below

Ascension - **Day 3:**
Dry Land, Grain and Fruit

Testing - **Day 4:**
Ruling Lights

Maturity - **Day 5:**
Birds and Fish

Conquest - **Day 6:**
Animals and Man

Glorification - **Day 7:**
Rest and Rule

Feasts

Creation - **Sabbath:**
Weekly Rest - House of Israel

Division - **Passover:**
Sin Removed (external Law)

Ascension - **Firstfruits:**
Israel as Priest

Testing - **Pentecost:**
Israel as King

Maturity - **Trumpets:**
Israel as Prophet

Conquest - **Atonement:**
Sin Removed (internal Law)

Glorification - **Booths (Ingathering):**
Annual Rest - House of All Nations

Dominion

Creation - **Genesis:**
Israel called from the Nations

Division - **Exodus:**
Israel cut from the Nations

Ascension - **Leviticus:**
Israel Presented to God (Man)

Testing - **Numbers:**
Israel Threshed (People)

Maturity - **Deuteronomy:**
Israel Reassembled (Army)

Conquest - **Joshua:**
The Nations cut from the Land

Glorification - **Judges:**
Israel among the Nations

Sacrifice

Creation - **Called:**
Animal Chosen

Division - **Sanctified:**
Animal Separated / Sacrifice Cut

Ascension - **Presented:**
Sacrifice Lifted Onto Altar
Sacrifice Awaits

Testing - **Purified:**
Holy Fire Descends

Maturity - **Transformed:**
Clouds of Fragrant Smoke

Conquest - **Vindicated:**
The Savor Accepted by God

Glorification - **Sent:**
Reconciliation and Reunion

GOD'S KITCHEN

Tabernacle

Creation - **Ark of the Covenant:**
The Law Written on Stone

Division - **Veil:**
The Face of God Veiled

Ascension -
Bronze Altar
The Adamic Body Formed
and Golden Table:
The Face of Adam Presented

Testing - **Lampstand:**
The Eyes of God Opened

Maturity - **Incense Altar:**
The Evian Body Formed

Conquest - **Sacrifices & High Priest:**
The Face of God Unveiled

Glorification - **Shekinah:**
The Law Written on Flesh

Covenant

TRANSCENDENCE
Creation - **Initiation:**
God begins a new era in history

HIERARCHY
Division - **Delegation:**
He sets apart His representatives

ETHICS (LAW)
Ascension - **Presentation:**
Law is given to them

Testing - **Purification:**
Law is opened to them

Maturity - **Transformation:**
Law is received by them

SANCTIONS (OATH)
Conquest - **Vindication:**
His representatives submit to
God's blessing or cursing

SUCCESSION
Glorification - **Representation:**
The faithful are commissioned as rulers
and given an inheritance in history

Work

Creation:
You wake from sleep

Division:
You go to work

Ascension:
You are given instructions

Testing:
You work unsupervised
Your faculties are tested

Maturity:
Work brings you prosperity
and wisdom

Conquest:
You return home

Glorification:
You eat and rest

Eating

Creation:
Your food is presented to you as the result of previous faithfulness

> **Division:**
> You cut it up or break it up

>> **Ascension:**
>> You lift it to your mouth with clean hands or culinary tools

>>> **Testing:**
>>> You chew it up and make a judgment upon it as you taste it ("Taste and see")

>> **Maturity:**
>> It is united with your body as either "plunder or plagues," a blessing or a curse

> **Conquest:**
> The food is "divided." The waste is expelled, and washed away or buried

Glorification:
The beneficial elements bring life *to* you, and obtain a new life *in* you

Food Laws - Head

ADAM'S PROHIBITION

Creation - **Initiation:**
Springs water the Land,
but there is no Man

> *Division* - **Delegation:**
> Adam is formed out of the dust,

> > *Ascension* - **Presentation:**
> > given a single, temporary
> > PROHIBITION, then broken
> > and opened to construct Eve

> > > *Testing* - **Purification:**
> > > The serpent seduces Eve.
> > > Adam and Eve eat, and their
> > > eyes are opened

> > *Maturity* - **Transformation:**
> > The PROHIBITION is now
> > obsolete. They attempt to hide
> > their nakedness

> *Conquest* - **Vindication:**
> and are judged by the Lord. Innocent
> substitutes are de-formed

Glorification - **Representation:**
Instead of ingathering, there is scattering

Food Laws - Body

EVE'S PROHIBITIONS

Creation - **Initiation:**
Rivers of blood (genealogy and sacrifice) flow
from Eden but there is no mediatorial Man

Division - **Delegation:**
Israel is formed out of a barren
womb *(Circumcision)*,

Ascension - **Presentation:**
raised up and put into the Land.
They are given many temporary
PROHIBITIONS, then broken in
two, opened to build a new Body

Testing - **Purification:**
Christ defeats the serpent
and opens the Church's eyes

Maturity - **Transformation:**
The PROHIBITIONS become
obsolete. The Firstfruits Church is
robed in white, witnesses boldly,

Conquest - **Vindication:**
and Herodian worship is judged by the
Lord. Old Covenant Israel is de-formed
(un-Circumcision)

Glorification - **Representation:**
Under the Married Mediatorial Man, rivers of
living water flow out into all the nations

Law of Moses [1]

FORMING *(Head - Adam - Priest)*	FILLING *(Body - Eve - People)*
TRANSCENDENCE	
1	**2**
Word from God	Word to God
False Gods	*False Oath*
HIERARCHY	
3	**4**
Work	Land
Sabbath	*Father and Mother*
KNIFE ETHICS	***FIRE***
5	**6**
Murder	Adultery
Sons of God	*Daughters of Men*
SANCTIONS	
7	**8**
Stealing	False Witness
False Blessings	*False Curses*
SUCCESSION	
9	**10**
Coveting Shelter	Coveting the Sheltered
Formed House	*Filled House*

---

1 See *Bible Matrix II: The Covenant Key*, Chapter 4, for an explanation of why I have arranged the Ten Words in this fashion.

Law of Christ

Creation:
Jesus opened His mouth and taught them.
It was actually those with a humble spirit
who owned the Creation *(Sabbath)*

Division:
Those who set themselves apart and
mourned for the sins of the Land
would be comforted *(Passover)*

Ascension:
The obedient would inherit the
Land. Those who were hungry
and thirsty for righteousness
would be satisfied *(Firstfruits)*

Testing:
The merciful obtain mercy.
The pure in heart see God
(Pentecost)

Maturity:
The true sons of God are martyrs
for unity, peacemakers *(Trumpets)*

Conquest:
The prophets are accused and rejected
(Atonement)

Glorification:
Their reward is in heaven *(Booths)*

Sex

Creation:
Adam, as Word, initiates the act of
procreation that will change history

> **Division:**
> Eve is chosen and cherished. Adam's
> self-sacrifice in foreplay leads to...
>
> > **Ascension:**
> > arousal of the holy fire of
> > desire. He "overshadows" Eve
> >
> > > **Testing:**
> > > Man and Woman are
> > > united as "Ish" and "Isha"
> >
> > **Maturity:**
> > Climax: Adam's is singular
> > and Eve's is "multiple."
> > Eve is "filled with a swarm"
>
> **Conquest:**
> As Eve was chosen by Adam, so an
> ovum as "Body" chooses her "Head"

Glorification:
Passion subsides and there is godly rest

Gestation

Creation:
As with the Sabbath, the pattern of the
sexual act prefigures the act of gestation.
Of many ova, one is chosen

Division:
called out,

Ascension:
freed from barrenness by Adamic
fertilization, (the flow of blood is
stopped) (Single Coded Cell)

Testing:
and "opened" in cell
division (Code Applied).

Maturity:
Eve "shines" in pregnancy.
Multiplication leads to a new
body (Multiplied Coded Cells)

Conquest:
Birth pangs, water and blood. The child
is "divided" from its mother and the
"old house," the placenta, is expelled

Glorification:
The pain of childbirth subsides and there is
godly rest, a new family, a "larger tent"

History

Creation - **Adam to Noah:**
World united as one blood

Division - **Abraham to Joseph:**
World divided by blood
(Circumcision)

Ascension - **Moses to AD30:**[2]
Centralized priesthood
EARTHLY MEDIATORS

Testing - **Christ:**
The harvest begins

Maturity - **Christ to AD70:**[3]
Centralized priesthood
HEAVENLY MEDIATORS

Conquest - **AD70 to final judgment:**
World divided by water
(Baptism)

Glorification - **final judgment:**
World united by one Spirit

2   The death of Christ.
3   The destruction of the Jewish Temple and the city of Jerusalem.

And their eyes were opened...

Both Yahweh and Satan desire
to open our eyes to good and to evil.
Both call us to "taste and see."
Both taste good.
But only Yahweh *is* good.

The eschatological feast is the one where the intimacy prefigured by marriage is actually between *every member of the body,* and thus, not in this life. It is a festal variety beyond our current capacity.

1

Cooking as eschatology[1]

DELICIOUS SUPERFLUITY I

But while they still did not believe for joy, and marveled, He said to them, "Have you any food here?" So they gave Him a piece of a broiled fish and some honeycomb. And He took it and ate in their presence. (Luke 24:42 NKJV)

THANKS TO DOUG WILSON'S RECOMMENDATIONS OF IT, one of the books I took with me to hospital (to undergo heart surgery) was *The Supper of the Lamb* by Robert Farrar Capon. It is a mouth-watering fusion of cookbook and theology, pushing the idea of multi-disciplinary insights to the outer limit. But then, we moderns don't have such biblical horizons, do we? We refuse to see the world as the Bible reveals it to us.

---

1   The study of the "final things," including death, the destiny of humanity, the Second Coming and the Last Judgment.

We now believe that tearing it into molecules and atoms is the path to truth. As Wilson once observed, the atheist draws the Christian to a close-up of the microscopic elements that make up a tree and says, smugly, "Where is your God now?" Instead of discovering what (or whom) the end is to which the world is pointing, we are fixated on the protological, on Creation (and that usually with corrupt motives). Ultimately, despite the advances in medicine and other technologies, this is a feast for fools. It is a misinterpretation of the world that makes us outwardly fat but leaves us inwardly famished.

For Capon, however, gathering the raw elements of the world together into sauces, sausages, soups and strudels is a facet of Man's imaging of the work of God in the world, the work of *Glorification*.

On a certain couple who despised variety as "inefficient," killjoys who considered as progress the development of a food pill, he comments:

> Into outer darkness then with the pill-roller and his wife. They have missed the point of the world; they are purely and simply mad. Man invented cooking before he thought of nutrition. To be sure, food keeps us alive, but that is only its smallest and most temporary work. Its eternal purpose is to furnish our sensibilities against the day when we shall sit down at the heavenly banquet and see how gracious the Lord is. Nourishment is necessary

only for a while; what we shall need forever is taste.

Pills indeed! Some day, no doubt, the dreadful offspring of that hapless couple will invent flavorless capsules which, when swallowed, will give the user a complete command of any desired language. Let us hope only that when he does, the sane among us will lobby for a law to keep such people from writing poems. Language is no utilitarian abstraction; English, French, Greek and Latin are concrete delights, relishings by which the flavor of words and syntax are rolled over the tongue. And so in their own way are all the declensions and conjugations of beef, lamb, pork, and veal. Food is the daily sacrament of unnecessary goodness, ordained for a continual remembrance that the world will always be more delicious than it is useful. Necessity is the mother only of cliché. It takes playfulness to make poetry.[2]

Capon doesn't despise simplicity whatsoever, but even his simplicity is artful and crafty. There is a time to fast and a time to feast. This, too, is eschatological. Witness the new worship established in Daniel as he refuses the king's food and requests Edenic "seeds." The culinary culmination of this Restoration process, Daniel to Esther, (as Adam to Eve), was constant feasting, and it is indeed a picture of all of history. As Jordan observes, men are protological.

2   Robert Farrar Capon, *The Supper of the Lamb: A Culinary Reflection*, p. 40.

Adam dies. That is his ministry. Women are eschatological. They are "resurrection bodies." They live longer and bear children. They are Covenant *Succession*.

The Torah is full of laws regarding food and sex. The food laws were pedagogical. They passed away.[3] Might the laws concerning sex also pass away? How many times do the godless point out the Christian's illogical cherry-picking of Leviticus?

God began with a green world, collecting herbs, cutting us up like raw foods, the seeds in the Garden. Noah, a wise judge, moved the world to meat. Moses introduced more elaborate preparation in the Levitical Laws. Aaron's two sons were unworthy and consumed, but the Babylonian fire glorified the three Jews and made them an acceptable offering.

"...and the Lord smelled a soothing aroma."

Finally, Jesus put True Fire on the Altar. He called His wedding party and His guests are now being gathered. The eschatological feast is the one where the intimacy prefigured by marriage is fulfilled between *every member of the body,* and thus, not in this life. It is a festal variety

---

3   In the Bible Matrix, the temporary command to Adam corresponds "fractally" with the food laws in the big picture (see *Bible Matrix,* pp. 20-21). Also, Jordan observes that the forbidden animals were in most cases the more "glorious" ones.

beyond our current capacity, kept in store for the resurrection body, a multitude in a single Bride. As in Eden, a disobedient reach for future glory, for things that God has temporarily withheld due to our immaturity, brings plagues instead of plunder. This applied to food and it still applies to sex. Manna, like hospital food, is certainly a gift from God, but it is temporary. Its purpose is to humble us.

There is no marriage in heaven, at least not as we know it. There will be no longer any need for nourishment, for family, for abstinence and sacrifice. Just as glorious cities now plunder and devour the world, the final glory fulfills all the carnal pictures and leaves behind the pedagogical husk. We fast and sacrifice that we may feast. For now, the best things, the most delectable, the wine, the sweet crispy fat, the cigars, are to be enjoyed only in moderation. Constant extravagance kills us. These things are too intoxicating for our feeble tents. Enjoying them requires the wisdom of Solomon. Addicts are fools like Adam who inappropriately crave the God-moderated excesses of the Feast of Tabernacles every day.

"...all the fat is the Lord's."

Yet, these "forbidden" things are God-given tastes of future glory. The best wine is yet to come. In that day, we will eat without devouring; and we will know as we are known. Relationship cures addiction.

On Communion as a pattern for life

"The difference between the wicked and the righteous is whether or not we give thanks as we take hold of the world."

—James B. Jordan, *Ritual and Typology.*
biblicalhorizons.wordpress.com

The suffering of the saints is not the mark of an irredeemable world, but the very means of its transformation.

2

Postmillennial suffering

...since we are surrounded
by so great a cloud of witnesses...
(Hebrews 12:1)

TO DEFEAT SATAN IS TO EXPOSE HIS LIES TO THE TRUTH — to *unmask* him. We see lots of unmaskings in the Bible. Many of these use the saints as bait. The true natures of Pharaoh, of Job's accusers, and of Haman and the enemies of God in Esther, were all exposed when God's people became weak. A corpse always brings out the "dirty birds" (Matthew 24:28), the "Edomites"—false brothers—waiting to loot a razed Jerusalem.

The suffering of the saints and the defeat of God's enemies both become a public spectacle. The destruction of Pharaoh's army, Job's "resurrection" and the two-day humiliation of the "new Amalekites" from India to Ethiopia all picture for us the work of Christ on the cross, where death was swallowed up in victory. He turned the electric chair of the day into the throne of God.

Then the body, the Church, followed the head in making a shameful public spectacle of the powers-that-were (Colossians 2:15; 1 Corinthians 4:9; Hebrews 10:33). Such was said of Nero, who orchestrated his own public spectacles:

> Mockery of every sort was added to their [Christians'] deaths. Covered with the skins of beasts, they were torn by dogs and perished, or were nailed to crosses, or were doomed to the flames. These served to illuminate the night when daylight failed. Nero had thrown open the gardens for the spectacle, and was exhibiting a show in the circus, while he mingled with the people in the dress of a charioteer or drove about in a chariot. Hence, even for criminals who deserved extreme and exemplary punishment there arose a feeling of compassion; for it was not, as it seemed, for the public good, but to glut one man's cruelty, that they were being punished. (Tacitus, *Annales*, 15, 44.)

This is the difference between amillennial and postmillennial definitions of suffering.[1] The suffering of the saints is not the mark of an irredeemable world, but the very means of its transformation.[2]

Job was a righteous, priestly king who suffered for

---

1 Amillennials believe that the nations will increase in godlessness before the return of Christ. Postmillennials believe that the Gospel of Christ will transform the nations substantially before His return.
2 An insight from James B. Jordan's lecture on Romans 8, available from www.wordmp3.com

that righteousness. When his royal advisors became his accusers *(satans)*, Job rightly refused to be scapegoated, to be coerced into giving them the confession they desired.[3] As a public spectacle of innocent suffering, he shamed the powers. The wonder of this refusal by an innocent victim to shoulder the blame is that whether he lives or dies, a new culture forms around his testimony. This is why Christian martyrdom expands the kingdom.

The sufferings of Christ and the saints aren't merely for the sake of making more converts; they eventually bring evil powers tumbling down and transform *this* world for Christ. It was the suffering of Christians which dis-empowered pagan Rome and then "Holy" Rome. A perfect illustration of this principle is the crowds of underground Christians who finally came out and risked their lives to march through the streets just before the fall of the Soviet Union, carrying placards that said, "We forgive you." After decades of suffering, they publicly shamed the powers.

More recently, the houses and churches of Christians in northern India were destroyed by demonized Hindus. Some saints were even hacked to pieces. While Christians worked and prayed to bring the persecution to an end, the

---

3   See James B. Jordan, *Was Job an Edomite King?*, Biblical Horizons Nᵒs 130 & 131, www.biblicalhorizons.com

nations saw the lie of Hinduism exposed for the counterfeit that it is. The long term result will be an expansion of the Kingdom of God in that territory.

Indeed, the only reason we Christians in the West are free is because of the sufferings and deaths of saints who transformed the world before us. Christendom was, and will only ever be, bought with service, suffering and blood.

> I think that God has exhibited us apostles as last of all, like men sentenced to death, because we have become a spectacle to the world, to angels, and to men.
> (1 Corinthians 4:9)

The Great Commission was not a command to get people to heaven. It is a strategy focused on transforming the nations through union with Christ and His suffering.

Have we lost sight of working and suffering for a *tangible* Christian future? The priestly ministry and intercessory throne of Christ was earned—perfected—by suffering and death for the purpose of transfiguring *this* world, not the next.

A two-edged sword

"Some today emphasize the suffering
and external weakness of the Kingdom
so much that they deny the Biblical
promises of victory in history, while
those who emphasize victory seldom
emphasize sufficiently the role of
suffering and martyrdom in the
advancement of the Kingdom."

— James B. Jordan, *Biblical Horizons Mission Statement.*

REAPERS AT WORK

The "last days"
are only ever
the last days of
the old order.

3

The whole bloody Bible

ENDING THE FALSE DICHOTOMY OF BLOOD AND SPIRIT

THE OLD TESTAMENT IS A BLOODY BOOK. Beginning with Adam's "dissection" for the construction of Eve and the animals the Lord slew to make tunics, the Old Covenant ends with the massacre of saints under Herod and Nero (Revelation 14), and then the massacre of the unbelieving Jews under Vespasian and Titus.

The Land is always bought with blood. Sitting around John Piper's "eschatology round table" in September 2009, the premillennialist (Jim Hamilton) and the amillennialist (Sam Storms) had problems understanding that Doug Wilson's postmillennialism is not about a sudden Utopia on earth. It is about buying the world with blood—*this* world. Yes, there is martyrdom, but then there is Christian culture.

Following the example of Christ, the "engine" of post-millennialism is a willingness to die because, although you have one eye on heaven, the other eye is focused on the glory that can be bought for God *on earth*. Like Wycliffe's prayer from the stake that God would open the eyes of the King of England, it is "visionary suffering."

Blood is only ever a *foundation*. Spirit follows. The Law kills but the Spirit gives life. The slaughter of saints actually disarms the old worship, and Christianity fills the void. The atrocities of communism in China and Mongolia cast the ancient demons out of the house and the Holy Spirit finds it swept and garnished. He fills the vacuum like a mighty, rushing wind.

So, the Reformers didn't need to *keep* dying. The Firstfruits (first century) Church didn't *keep* dying. The "last days" are only ever the last days of the old order. A New Jerusalem is *formed* on the blood of the apostles and prophets—but then it is also *filled!* My friend Matthew Moffitt writes:

> If you had to put your finger on what caused the rise of the church in the Roman world (and beyond) in the first four centuries AD, what would you suggest? Miracles (as Eusebius suggests)? The blood of the martyrs (as Tertullian suggests)? I'd be inclined to follow sociologist Rodney Stark's suggestion that it was through relational networks of family and friends.

(Rodney Stark would also argue that it was Christian behavior that made it so attractive, particularly its treatment of women.)

According to Emperor Julian (b. 331/332, d. 363), the last pagan emperor of the Roman Empire, the rise of Christianity in its first four centuries—by the end of which at least half the empire was Christian—was due to the distinctive behavior of Christians (D. B. Hart lists these as temperance, gentleness, lawfulness, and acts of supererogatory kindness) which were visible and appealing to their non-Christian neighbors.

Julian wrote: "It is [the Christians'] philanthropy towards strangers, the care they take of the graves of the dead, and the affected sanctity with which they conduct their lives that have done most to spread their atheism." [1, 2]

Of course, all of this comes back to *totus Christus*: the "head first" pattern in the Bible.[3] The head is blood (circumcision), the body is Spirit (baptism). Saints die as seeds, as Christ did, and their deaths allow a great harvest. But that harvest is characterized by community life. The

---

1 Matthew Moffitt, *Growth of the Old Atheism,* absurdity-of-absurdities.blogspot.com.au

2 Julian, *Epistle 22 to Arsacius, the pagan priest of Galatia.* Quoted by D. B. Hart in *Atheist Delusions: The Christian Revolution and Its Fashionable Enemies.*

3 *Totus Christus* is a Latin expression which means "the whole Christ," that is, Christ as the head and the Church as His body.

living stones of the bridal city have the Spirit as mortar. This brand new culture, a new leaven, is impossible without the cutting off of the old.

So, the blood of the martyrs is indeed the seed of the Church, but Tertullian's famous quote only gives us half the picture. Stark, however, only gives us the *other* half of the picture. But we need both sides. There must be blood *and* Spirit.

The problem with our "post-Christian" culture is that the harvest here has mostly ended. Our anemic theology is all about "love," a love defined by the needs of man, a love limited to the comforts of fellowship and community. As with Rome's fixation on Mary, we desire only fragrant Eve, and not bloody Adam, because Eve is soft and comforting. Our faith has become effeminate.

We need new blood, new foundations. The extension of the government of Christ requires attendance to the altar. The bloody Old Testament is now foreign to us, so we must continually revisit the death of Adam.[4]

True, culture-changing community can only be achieved again when Christians are willing to be Adam-seeds. We need those bloody foundations, and teaching the whole bloody Bible is the place to start. Without the shedding of blood there is no remission of sins, no nearbringing to the throne.[5] This shedding begins with faithfulness to Bible and Table and Mission, bloody *Word,* bloody *sacrament* and bloody *government* (church discipline and state justice) until the whole world knows the power of His resurrection.

> *Of the increase of his government and of peace there will be no end, on the throne of David and over his kingdom, to establish it and to uphold it with justice and with righteousness from this time forth and forevermore. The zeal of the Lord of hosts will do this.* (Isaiah 9:7)

4   I highly recommend James Jordan's *Crisis, Opportunity and the Christian Future*, which the publisher describes as follows:
> We are witnessing the end of Western Civilization. The present crisis in our culture is the greatest since the first century. Many commentators on the present scene believe that the entire world is moving into a period of "neo-tribalism."
> In this striking book, theologian James B. Jordan argues that this cultural change is part of God's ongoing plan for humanity, the plan by which the Holy Spirit grows God's daughter, humanity, into a fit bride for His Son.
> The present crisis provides a tremendous opportunity for the Christian Church to challenge and transform the world as never before. Here, Jordan points to how this can be done.
> While many view the present crisis with dismay, and are looking backwards to older traditions, Jordan argues that God is calling us forward, and that the Bible points the way.

5   James Jordan suggests that instead of sacrifice or offering, a better translation of the word *qorban* would be "nearbringing". "The English 'sacrifice' tends to connote the idea of giving something up for someone else. That has little if anything to do with *qorban*. 'Offering' tends to connote a gift, which again has nothing to do with *qorban*. The word means to draw near, to get into close relationship with someone, and it is used only in relationship to God. We do not worship God by giving Him anything, for He needs nothing. We do not worship God by giving up anything good, for He is the one who has given us all good things. We worship God by drawing near to Him." James B. Jordan, Leviticus 1:2, Biblical Horizons N° 143, www.biblicalhorizons.com

As we become
living sacrifices,
the Sacraments
take on flesh.

4

Love in the abstract

HOSPITALITY AS WORSHIP

Come, you who are blessed by my Father ... For I was
hungry and you gave me food, I was thirsty and you gave
me drink, I was a stranger and you welcomed me, I was
naked and you clothed me, I was sick and you visited me,
I was in prison and you came to me. (Matthew 25:34-36)

IN AN AFFLUENT SOCIETY, THE DEBATE BETWEEN WELFARE and
generosity gravitates towards cold, hard cash. But Jesus'
call goes beyond our bank balances into our hearts and
even (gasp!) into our homes. Steve Wilkins writes:

> The love of the world is an abstraction, and one that is
> very easy to talk about. Anyone can say, "I love the
> poor," and most of them can even be sincere. But they
> mean that they love the poor whom they do not know.
> They love the poor across town, who will never come to
> their door. They love the poor whom they will never
> touch.

We all know that our congressmen and senators "love" the disadvantaged, but have they ever met them or invited them into their homes? Only then would they understand how difficult it can often be to deal with different kinds of people, and how much they can try one's love.

It is easy to love people with whom one has no contact, and the world is all too full of this abstract and worthless love. This love does not care to actually help others, aside from perhaps guiltily throwing a bit of money at them.

The biblical love God commands is never merely a subjective emotion; it is always manifested physically, tangibly, and visibly. Hospitality is a concrete, down-to-earth test of our love for God and for His people. One can talk all he pleases about concern for the weak, lonely, crippled and difficult members of the body, but he does not love them until he has proved that concern with action.[1]

This "tangible" love flows directly out of the Covenant "week." It begins with God calling us to an initial shelter, the Sabbath, which sets the pattern for life. In the **Word**, God gives us the blueprint. *Audible.* As we become living sacrifices, the **Sacraments** take on flesh. God opens for

---

1   Steve Wilkins, *Face to Face: Meditations on Friendship and Hospitality,* pp. 100-101.

the world a Holy Place, somewhere safe. *Visible.* As the world sees an open door and responds, the people sheltering under the wings of God themselves become a shelter, extending the **Government** of the Spirit. *Practical.* The process ends with *Tabernacles,* that is, a bigger tent and a better rest.[2]

This process of shelter, enlarging the tent, is Covenantal, Creational and Festal. It is the nature of true Dominion. The most effective but neglected "front line" of evangelism in your church might be simple hospitality.

The world's abstract love can never be a lasting shelter because it is not personal or truly sacrificial. True hospitality is liturgical. It begins in the abstract but does not remain so because it *instructs.* It bears "children." Those who come to the Church for shelter are themselves destined to become shelter. The Covenants of God always leave a legacy.

---

2   For a diagram of this process, see *Bible Matrix II: The Covenant Key*, p. 34. The book includes some examples of how Jesus turns this pattern on its head in His condemnation of the Covenant failure and inhospitality of Israel's leadership.

If we insist on a policy of "Eat Local," and confuse the Lord's Table with the Love Feast, the Gentiles eventually come, not as *guests,* but as *scavengers.*

5

Eat local and die

TURNING THE TABLES

For wherever the carcass is, there the eagles will be gathered together. (Matthew 24:28 NKJV)

TABERNACLES, AS THE FINAL HARVEST OF THE YEAR (grapes and olives), was also called "Ingathering." In Matthew 24, Jesus employs Israel's heptamerous festal calendar (Leviticus 23) as a deep literary structure, and He uses this pattern to make a terrifying joke centered upon food.

As a holy priesthood, we are to be eaten by the world. But there are two Tables and we often confuse them.

PRIESTS AND KINGS

The Aaronic priesthood was authorized to *make* sacrifices, to *eat* sacrifices, and thus *be* sacrifices, standing face-to-face as mediators *for Israel,* as Facebread, the broken Adam, in the very presence of God. After national cleansing, Israel herself, as the second table, was then to be bread *for the nations.* Mostly, however, they hoarded the bread.

Passover was a Table for Jews only. The Gentiles could only look on. James Jordan writes:

> In order for a stranger to eat Passover, he had to circumcise himself and his household (Exodus 12:45-49). If he did so, he became "like a native of the *land*" (v. 48). We are so accustomed to connecting Passover with the Lord's Supper that it seems strange to consider that perhaps Passover was only for the priestly people, but such was the case. Converted gentiles were not to eat of it unless they were circumcised, and thereby were incorporated into the seed line of Abraham. Did this exclude them from salvation? No, it only excluded them from priestly duties. Did it make them second class citizens? Only in the eyes of the Pharisees. Biblically speaking, their downstream cultural labors in Havilah were just as important as Israel's sanctuary task. After all, if everyone had become an Israelite, then who would mine the gold of Havilah? Who would bring it to the sanctuary? Israel had its task, and the converted nations had theirs.
>
> Passover was not a sign of salvation, but of *coming* salvation. Passover constituted Israel a "peculiar" people, particularly redeemed by God, and given a special priestly task. How were the gentiles related to

Passover? By watching it, and putting faith in it. Someday, according to the promise of the covenant, they would be let in the House. For now, they were to stand at the doors and windows and look in. They watched the peculiar people eat the Passover, and they trusted that God would save them as well. They watched the peculiar priestly people circumcise their children, and they trusted that the benefits of that act were theirs as well.[1]

The very purpose of Israel from the beginning, besides carrying the promised "Seed", was to be a holy witness to Gentiles, a blessing to the nations. Unlike Passover, Tabernacles *was* a Table for the nations. Seventy bulls were sacrificed for the seventy nations listed in Genesis 10. Every year was to end in a combined Jew-Gentile "Godfest." Gentiles were invited to join in the celebrations, picturing the reunion fulfilled in the first century.

The Jewish leaders, however, abused the "talent" God had given them. Magnifying the Mosaic food laws, they forbade even eating with Gentiles. They taught the Jews that the very ministry God had given them would *defile* them. Instead, their refusal to eat with Gentiles was the outflow of what *truly* defiled them (Matthew 23:25-26).

---

1   James B. Jordan, *The Sociology of the Church*, p. 103.

After rejecting the Jew-Gentile Church, the defining feast for the Herods' "renewed" Judaism and finished Temple was *the biggest Passover ever* in AD65. Millions of lambs were sacrificed. In response, Jesus turned what was intended to be their greatest blessing into an eternal curse.

BURSTING THE ELITIST BUBBLE

In Isaiah 49:26, the Lord promised to take vengeance upon Israel's oppressors.

> I will make your oppressors eat their own flesh, and they shall be drunk with their own blood as with wine. Then all flesh shall know that I am the Lord your Savior, and your Redeemer, the Mighty One of Jacob.

Peter Leithart writes:

> If we want Yahweh as our Redeemer, we have to learn to love the God who stuffs our enemies full of their own flesh. There is an eye-for-eye justice here.
>
> The nations eat Israel's flesh and drink her blood, and Yahweh reciprocates: Flesh for flesh, blood for blood. Nations that sacrifice the innocent become their own sacrificial food. God gives them over to a horror movie Eucharist.
>
> Here we see the grim irony of violence. Israel's enemies thought they were making themselves fat on Israel's flesh. They thought they were trampling Israel, but they discover they were trampling themselves. To

their dismay, they realize the arm they have been gnawing is their own.[2]

The Lord had freed Israel from Babylon, but now Israel herself had become a new Babylon. The curses that once fell upon Israel's oppressors now fell upon her.

Jesus' "Tabernacles" irony in Matthew 24:28 concerns the nature of the Holy Table that had become "a snare" (Psalm 69:22; Romans 11:9-10). Since the Jews would not invite Gentiles to eat at this Table that God had prepared, God brought Gentiles to the Table anyway.

Roman armies besieged Jerusalem in AD66. The walls held the outsiders at bay for three and a half years, during which those trapped inside ran out of food. Many Jews starved and some even resorted to cannibalism. Finally, the Gentiles broke in and the entire city was devoured.

Because the Jewish rulers and their followers would not be bread for the nations, Jesus made *them* the meat on the table. They refused to serve, so they would be "served." Both tables, priestly and kingly, were now defiled.

The Old Covenant curses fell for the last time and brought about the end of the Circumcision—forever. Israel "according to the flesh" went up in smoke.

2   Peter J. Leithart, *Eucharistic Meditation,* Sunday, November 4, 2012 www.firstthings.com/blogs/leithart

There is no longer Jew nor Gentile. The two tables, however, were not destroyed. They were transfigured. Dr. Leithart continues:

> God prepares two tables, and you're going to be at one of them. For unrepentant oppressors, brutal tyrants, cruel husbands, those who war against the saints, He prepares a cannibal feast. For those who receive unworthily, this table becomes that cannibal feast.[3]

Just as AD70 was the end of the Jew/Gentile bipolarity, this age is leading us to the final great Tabernacles, the end of the believer/unbeliever division. Until then, the saints are the "sacramental bridge" between Word and Government.

The Lord's Table is exclusive. All are invited to eat, but only on very specific Covenantal terms. Repentance, baptism and membership of a church (accountability) are required. Our approach is a call for judgment upon us, for fire to fall upon us as sacrifices. We are slain and resurrected for the world every week. This is not the time or place to sit around informally at café tables. "Café Church" brings confusion and invites scattering. Church, liturgy and church music are supposed to be set apart—sanctified—from the world. In the New Covenant gathering, God's people eat with God on God's terms.

---

3   Leithart.

But outside of this, we *must* be eating with unbelievers. We eat with them in their houses and ours on *their* terms. That is the place for "Café Church" hospitality and informality. As the Lord is food on our Table, we are the food on the godless tables of the nations.

In their proselytizing, the Jews got their two Tables mixed up, and very often we do too. Jewish exclusivism always brought barrenness, scarcity. It eventually left the righteous begging for bread. But when Israel was faithful, the Gentiles brought their glory into the kingdom. (Note this exact scenario in Acts 11:28-30).

EITHER WAY, WE ARE EATEN

If we insist on a policy of "Eat Local", and magnify the Lord's Table to the exclusion of the Love Feast, the Gentiles eventually come, not as guests, but as *scavengers*. They tear up the Temple stones looking for melted gold. Our desolate church buildings become cafés, bed and breakfasts, and hair salons.

The saints gather not merely in the hope that *we* are sheltered (Passover), but that *we ourselves might become* a corporate shelter (Tabernacles), a great tree providing a spiritual covering and spiritual food for all the world. The Lord's Table is a blessing but it is a means to an end—a single Table at the Great Feast of the Resurrection.

Drinking blood

"When you drink wine [in Communion] you are volunteering for death; you are accepting martyrdom."

— James B. Jordan, *Worship*, Lectures series, 2009.

The child questions the command with "But why?" The father replies, "Because I am your father." Adam's sin was relational.

6

Knowing as we are known

If you love me, you will keep my commandments.

(John 14:15)

PETER LEITHART writes:

How do we know things? Experimentation, deduction, observation?

In Genesis, knowledge is first associated with two things—with food and with sex. There is a tree of the knowledge of good and evil, whose fruit opens the eyes of Adam and Eve so that they perceive that they are naked. Then Adam knows his wife and she conceives Cain.

If we want a strictly biblical answer: Knowledge is eating. Knowledge is sex.[1]

It seems Dr Leithart is having a go at the modern approach to science and philosophy: the belief that true

---

1   Peter J. Leithart, *Knowledge*, www.leithart.com

knowledge is only possible for those who are detached, dispassionate and unbiased. To *observe* reality in truth, the scientist must *remove* himself from it. "The world is not a sphere of relationships in which we participate. Rather, it is an object upon which we work."

In his lectures on Rosentock-Huessy at the 2008 Biblical Horizons Conference, Leithart says:

> The slogan of the Middle Ages was the slogan of Augustine and of Anselm: *credo ut intelligam,* "I believe that I may understand." Faith comes first. And faith seeks understanding.
>
> But the slogan of the modern world is the Cartesian slogan, *cogito ergo sum,* "I think therefore I am." This detached ego, trying to push away all tradition and all learning that it has gotten from elsewhere, to establish a foundation for his own existence in his own thought, is the slogan of modern philosophy.
>
> Rosenstock-Huessy doesn't see either of these slogans as inherently wrong. But he proposes a new slogan that transcends both, *respondeo etsi mutabor,* "I respond, although I shall be changed." [2]

Now finding it difficult to assess anything outside the *head-and-body* Dominion paradigm that is inherent in Scripture, I would say there are *two* kinds of eating and *two* kinds of sex.

---

2 Eugene Rosenstock-Huessy, "Farewell to Descartes" in *I Am an Impure Thinker.*

Initially, we are offered the Tree of Life and are joined in marriage *(Ascension)*. The first commandment is always an initiation "with a promise." It is a test of *obedience* to a limited revelation. It is Covenant. It is bread. It is priestly faith. It is an altar with four bloodied horns. There are grapes, but grapes are only a *promise* of wine, a promise that requires faith. *I believe.*

Then, we eat from the Tree of Wisdom as a new body *(Glorification)*. The marriage is no longer merely between individuals. Through obedience it becomes the animating spirit, that is, it is made *corporate*. It is a union between Judah and Israel, Jew and Gentile and, eventually, heaven and earth. It is Covenant *Succession*. It is wine. It is kingly sight, that is, sound judgment. It is a mountain with four living rivers. It is Shekinah.[3] *I understand.*

This process of promise and fulfillment is found in the popular proverb concerning the choice between giving a man a fish and teaching him *how* to fish. It is the difference between welfare and wealth. A Covenant takes people from being those who need shelter to those who can provide shelter—from childhood to adulthood.

We see this process in the grape haul in Exodus and Israel actually possessing—*inheriting by faith*—the

---

3   The Shekinah is the glory of God in His house, signifying a union between heaven and earth, prefiguring the day when man "sees" God.

vineyards of Canaan. Relatively speaking, the first "knowledge" is a betrothal. It is designed to grow obsolete. It is temporary because it is a test of relationship. Israel did not believe the promise. Israel failed the test of faithfulness.

> Children, obey your parents in the Lord, for this is right. "Honor your father and mother" (this is the first commandment with a promise), "that it may go well with you and that you may live long in the land." (Ephesians 6:1-3)

A promise concerning the future comes with a command. Very often, the child questions the command with "But why?" The father replies, "Because I am your father." Adam's sin was not merely legal; it was also relational.

These two degrees of knowledge—taste and feast—correspond to the Two Tables, the priest-only Passover and the all-welcome Tabernacles (Booths).[4] They also explain the transition from the temporary, humbling prohibitions of the Old Covenant dietary laws to our New Covenant liberties.

Sin is passionate but obedience is not dispassionate. It is a willingness to delay our gratification until God's time.

Once we gain a knowledge of the true heart of the

4   See the charts on pages 13 and 14.

Father in Christ, we serve Him out of love. His love constrains us not with cords and bars (commandments), but with a "holy lust," the purifying fire of the Spirit. This is the Law of Christ.

How do we stir up this passion? By "tasting" God *personally*, and then feasting *corporately*. Faith in God's character gives us a more mature taste, a hunger for things greater than we have known. It builds our relationship with our Father and our relationships with those in our sphere of influence. By faith, hungry thieves like Adam are filled with good things and become those willing to labor with their hands for others (Ephesians 4:28).

When we "get" this process of faith-then-sight, we move beyond the dark sayings of God and speak wisdom ourselves. We move from silence to song, from knowledge to wisdom, from the Law to Christ. We are weaned from fruit to become trees of righteousness. We ourselves *become* fathers. We finally know as we are known.

> *...you have come to know God,*
> *or rather to be known by God...*
> (Galatians 4:9)

> *And he said to them, "Follow me,*
> *and I will make you fishers of men."*
> (Matthew 4:19)

The end of the beginning

"Though Passover and Unleavened Bread
celebrate the completion of the exodus,
the exodus was only the beginning of
Israel's restoration."

—Peter J. Leithart, *Blessed Are the Hungry:
Meditations on the Lord's Supper,* p. 99.

In some
profound way,
knowledge is
singular but
wisdom is plural.

7
Knowledge and wisdom

DIGESTING THE LAW

"If you strike me down, I shall become more powerful than you can possibly imagine." —Ben Kenobi

HEROD AND VADER ARE MAGGOT-FILLED MEN. They are the living dead. Christ and Kenobi are willing to die. They become the dead living.

One factor the Bible Matrix continually brings out in its various occurrences throughout Scripture is the transformation of knowledge into wisdom through various kinds of death. In some profound way, knowledge is singular but wisdom is plural. The letter is given life in flesh and becomes capable of procreation.

The Lord gave Adam the knowledge of the Law, and Adam was expected to obey and become wise. His failure to confess his sin shows that he was no wiser than before.

In obedience, truth is digested, bringing death to self. A Covenant is always a bittersweet scroll. Then, by the Spirit, knowledge is resurrected as wisdom.

Moses silently received the Law on Sinai, then was tested as Israel's leader in the wilderness. In Deuteronomy, Moses sat enthroned as wisdom incarnate. After four decades of chewing on the Laws of the Covenant, the earthy, human, "singular" wisdom of the Egyptians (Acts 7:22) was slain by the Law and resurrected as the wisdom and knowledge of Christ—a marriage (Colossians 2:3). The Law kills precisely so that the Spirit may bring multiplied life. Resurrection is always plural. Through death, the one becomes many.

After Jesus was tempted in the wilderness, He gave the Sermon on the Mount. The male head falls into the ground and dies and the harvested (female) body is *sophia,* witnessing boldly on street corners (Proverbs 1:20). Hearing becomes doing. Wisdom is knowledge applied.

Men go to Bible College and they know it all. Then the Lord brings poverty, a marriage difficulty, a sick child, bereavement, betrayal, church schism, unemployment, a failed career or some temptation, and Gandalf the Grey is torn apart. God, why are you smashing up everything you built me for? Because I am frankincense, or garlic at the very least. Like these, and olives and grapes, *I was made to be crushed.* Gethsemane, after all, was an olive press. This is why novices are vulnerable leaders (1 Timothy 3:6).

Pentecost is the wilderness. It is the Lampstand, the eyes of God watching over us. Trumpets is the wisdom of Deuteronomy. It is the Incense Altar. We have been offered, torn apart, set on fire, and now ascend as holy smoke, a fragrant, mature wisdom that finally commands the respect of God's armies. We are broken so we can fill others. God makes us into a Promised Land which others can inherit. They see our fearless testimony and they fear. This is the beginning of their own wisdom.

The change we long for arrives in trials. As we suffer, our moral stink lessens. We become health to others instead of a canker. For the soft-hearted, every trial is an opportunity for greater service to the Body of Christ. For the saints, we must, when appropriate, allow ourselves to be cut down. Carnal victory is spiritual defeat.

> To have lawsuits at all with one another is already a defeat for you. Why not rather suffer wrong? Why not rather be defrauded? (1 Corinthians 6:7)

Fighting death makes you death incarnate. Vader learned this lesson in the end. He threw down his idol and submitted to ascension as smoke. He finally joined the rank of the heavenly elders as a bowl of incense. The dark father became a father of lights.

What men really desire
is to follow *other* men...

8

Omega males

*For I am already being poured out as a drink offering, and
the time of my departure has come.* (2 Timothy 4:6)

A BESTSELLING CHRISTIAN BOOK MISTAKENLY TELLS US TO BE
"wild at heart", which often results in passive wimps
looking into their dark, little, empty hearts to find selfish,
authoritarian rednecks.

There is nothing wrong with godly quests. Every
responsibility, every Covenant, is a quest of some sort. But
self-centered "identity quests" are not a solution. What
men really desire is to follow *other* men—godly elders
who are modeling Christ.

Bread is energizing Alpha food (morning); Wine is
intoxicating Omega food (evening).[1] Young men are
bread, ready to be broken. Breaking brings wisdom and
maturity. Old men are wisdom-wine, servant kings
poured out as "Sabbath rest" for the next generation.

---

1   I recommend James Jordan's lecture series, *One Life, Many Deaths,*
    available from www.wordmp3.com

The answer to bookish Christianity is not more Alpha Males (or less of them in some circles), but more of the Omega variety: fathers and mentors.

Food and history

"Food is both fuel and reward. We need food to get going, but good food is also our blessing for a job well done. Food is, thus, both alpha and omega, and our lives are encircled by food."

— James B. Jordan, *Studies in Food and Faith.*

If we endure
faithfully, we
bring gravity
with us out of
the grave.

9

True gravity

BECOMING THE FINGER OF GOD

The Spirit immediately drove him out into the wilderness.
(Mark 1:12)

Oswald Chambers said:

The first thing to do in examining the power that dominates me is to take hold of the unwelcome fact that I am responsible for being thus dominated. If I am a slave to myself, I am to blame because at a point away back I yielded to myself. Likewise, if I obey God I do so because I have yielded myself to Him.

Yield in childhood to selfishness, and you will find it the most enchaining tyranny on earth. There is no power in the human soul of itself to break the bondage of a disposition formed by yielding. Yield for one second to anything in the nature of lust (remember what lust is: "I must have it at once," whether it be the lust of the flesh or the lust of the mind)—once yield and though you may hate yourself for having yielded, you are a bondslave to that thing. There is no release in human power at all but only in the Redemption. You must yield yourself in utter humiliation to the only One Who can break the dominating power viz., the Lord Jesus Christ—"He hath anointed me . . . to preach deliverance to all captives."

You find this out in the most ridiculously small ways —"Oh, I can give that habit up when I like." You cannot, you will find that the habit absolutely dominates you because you yielded to it willingly. It is easy to sing, "He will break every fetter," and at the same time be living a life of obvious slavery to yourself. Yielding to Jesus will break every form of slavery in any human life.

"His servants ye are to whom ye obey." Romans 6:16 [1]

Peter Leithart notes that our word "devil" comes from the Greek word *ballo,* to throw. Dia-*bol*-ical makes the derivation more pronounced. Mark uses the word *ekballo* to describe the Spirit's action of throwing Jesus out, ejecting Him, into the wilderness to be tempted. He has been called as Moses, has passed through baptism as the Red Sea, ascended and been given the Law (in this case, the approval of the Father), and now, as Israel, He is "scattered" in the place of fiery serpents and surrounded by wild beasts. Where Israel failed, Christ succeeded, with the result that it was now Satan who was ejected by the

---

1 Oswald Chambers, *My Utmost For His Highest,* March 14th.

power of the Law—the Law made flesh, carved out on a human life. Filled with the Law by the Spirit, Jesus *became* the finger of God, a finger worthy of the holy eject button.

In the very next scene that Mark presents, Jesus *calls* the disciples, *teaches* with authority (as Moses) and then *ejects* a demon. The only reason He has such authority is because He Himself has passed through this test. Vindicated as Word-in-flesh, He can cast a demon *out* with a word. He has become the Ark on the move, scattering God's enemies.

This brings us back to Chambers' point. Jesus had passed through a death-and-resurrection in the wilderness and could now mediate this same process for the helpless—*for us.* As saints, when we fast and obey, Satan flees and we too are able to command him in the lives of others. But we cannot command him to whom we are still bowing for counterfeit kingdom.

Just as Jesus ejected Judas, He later ejected the demon from Judah (Israel). Her great Day of Atonement came in AD70. The finger of God chose the scapegoat and threw her into outer darkness, forever. The false church, the *totus diabolus,* on the last day, is thus, always, and by very definition, the scapegoat.

Whether the Lord tests us with food, sex, money, power, pride or some suffering like chronic illness or depression (in us or in a loved one), if we endure faithfully we bring gravity with us *out of* the grave. Life is suddenly more rich, more dense and our words more commanding. True *gravitas* comes in no other way, even in the life of Christ. He is lifted up so He can draw all men to Himself.

James Jordan observes that the possibility of kingdom without personal cost remains alluring to leaders who have not been through a death-and-resurrection experience. They are yet untempered. Great leadership comes from cruciform men; from those who have been broken as bread so that others may come and eat.

When it comes to spiritual ministry, without prior death in some form, we are prone to fail like the seven sons of Sceva (Acts 19:14). We can only overcome the world to the measure we have overcome it in ourselves. When we overcome, our words have power. Jesus is lifted up and people are drawn to us.

No pain is pointless

"No pastoral suffering is senseless.
No pastoral pain is pointless.
No adversity is absurd or meaningless.
Every heartache has its divine target in
the consolation of the saints, even when
we feel least useful."

—John Piper, *Brothers, We Are Not Professionals,* p. 140.

As my
grandfather said,
"The trials of life
will make you
bitter or better."
Either way, you
are food.

10

The expendables

or CALLING SECURITY

YEARS AGO, I REMEMBER A PREACHER LISTING for his audience all the sins that will make you prematurely old. I figured the second part of his sermon to us would be a list of all the benefits of Christian living that keep you young. Well, they are obvious. Don't tick the boxes in list one.

Very wisely, that's not what he gave us. He listed all the things the Lord expects of us, things that *also* make us prematurely old. His point was, grow old doing good, not evil.

Tying this to Jordan's bread and wine theology,[1] we understand that bread is made to be broken. Proud young men and women (as we were when I heard that sermon on growing old) won't stay that way. They *will* be broken. But one life offered can feed five thousand.

---

1   See James B. Jordan, *From Bread To Wine: Toward A More Biblical Liturgical Theology.* Available from www.biblicalhorizons.com

The media sells us a lifestyle of security. This is not biblical prudence. It is paranoia, a worldview without faith, where God and His people cannot be counted on to come to the rescue. The Bible is full of leaders and institutions who pulled back from being broken. God has no pleasure in them. It is the Tabernacle of Lamech, the Temple of the Herods, a hoarded bread that God fills with worms. Bread is not eternal. Manna is expendable.

Worldly dreams *will* be shattered. Christ calls us beyond that, to an expectation that we *will* be broken and poured out. In fact, He calls us to look for opportunities to become prematurely old, to lay down our lives for the next generation. We understand this of parenting. Do we understand this of discipling others?

I'm not talking about pastor's burnout. Paul knew how to disciple and delegate. Discipleship was a buffer against burnout. For sure, he had his failures, and he excommunicated them to bring about repentance. I'm talking about being a human shield, as Jesus was, standing between the curse and the cursed.

Adam's sin, as a proud young man with faculties even our most gifted youths can only dream about, was believing that he wasn't expendable. The single Law called him to be broken under it when tested. He seized a false security instead of becoming security. He was to be a priestly guard, a human firmament, a watchman, cut by the Word to create a sacred haven, a Holy Place. His failure sold us into slavery. As Doug Jones observes, the next question for everyone who is redeemed, in every possible station of life known to human beings, is "Whose freedom are you?"

Calculated risks are the order of the day. As with the Christian life, we don't set out to build a tower without adequate preparation and prudence. In parenting, in farming, in discipleship, we plant with an expectation, not a guarantee, of an increase. My point is that life in the flesh is expendable. Whatever we choose to spend it on, it will be spent. That is its very nature. It was never intended to last, not even in Eden. The natural would become spiritual. But the path to glory, to security for others (those in the house) and spiritual offspring (bringing in those outside the house), is expensive.

As a perceptive pastor once said, "If you want to be a highway into the kingdom for other people, don't be surprised when you get walked on." And as my grandfather said, "The trials of life will make you bitter or better." Either way, you are food.

> And I will very gladly spend and be spent for your souls; though the more abundantly I love you, the less I am loved. (2 Corinthians 12:15 NKJV)

The world sells us on youth and security, the glory of fresh bread somehow kept in suspended animation. But the world doesn't even believe the lie, not in the end, when the eulogies are read. When there is no reason to lie any more, even the world recognizes lives spent in such an honorable way.

Despite all the recent calls to be radical risk-takers and throw security to the wind, the Bible teaches us that security is good. That question, "Whose freedom are you?" helps us to discern between the guilt trips and the true calls to service. God doesn't call us all to live on the edge. There's nothing wrong with living a life of quiet faithfulness and nurturing of others. As we find our security in God by faith, He builds *us* into security for others.

We all have different gifts. Sometimes it takes more courage and strength to be non-radical, to be ordinary. Whether it's being radical, or just teaching your kids the Bible and being faithful at work, at home and at church, the goal is a legacy in history for God.

> *Cast your bread upon the waters,*
> *For you will find it after many days.*
> (Ecclesiastes 11:1)

Idolatry defined

"Idolatry is the attempt to squeeze out of a finite thing what only the infinite can provide. When we turn away from what the infinite God has supplied for us, we are forced to try to get more from the rest of the world than it can possibly provide. This is because God has set eternity in our hearts, and we seek out eternal things wherever we go, whatever we do."

— Doug Wilson, *The Peace is Yours to Keep*, www.dougwils.com

Doctor Jesus'
X-rays can be
a midlife crisis
or a call to
martyrdom.

11

Behind closed doors

HIDDEN IN PLAIN SIGHT

...who shut in the sea with doors, when it burst forth and issued from the womb? (Job 38:8 NKJV)

As with all good government, important kingdom decisions are carried out in private. This is pictured in many ways, not least in God's design of our everyday lives.

Living things have brains, guts and outsides. This is Word, Sacrament and Government. Word is intangible, but our emotions are communicated symbolically through our bodies. Facial expressions and body language are the response of the "Holy Place" to the "Most Holy" of our inner soul. Eyes are organs of judgment. Eyes are also the windows to the soul. The crystal sea is a window to heaven. The "outer court" interacts with the world and needs cleaning. Only clean stuff is allowed inside the "Holy Place."

The prayer closet is the place where we meet with God

95

in secret, and He rewards us openly, publicly. This applies to us as individuals and also corporately as a church. What happens here affects the history of the community and the world.

Marital relations happen behind closed doors. Everyone knows what happens in there, but sharing the details, or having sex in public, is taboo for all but the most reprobate. It is a private time where, among other things, Covenantal, governmental decisions are made, and God rewards us openly with offspring.

Gestation happens behind the "doors" of the womb. We are knit together in secret by God's miraculous government process. When the time comes, we pass from "death" to "life" through water and blood into a new world. Jesus referred to the last days as "birth pangs." The head was delivered at His ascension, and the body delivered in AD70 (the first resurrection). The complete "son of man" is Jesus and the Church. Revelation presents two women, the bride and the harlot. One delivers the man of sin (Cain) and the other, faithful Israel, finally delivers the *totus Christus*. This public vindication (the "revelation of the sons of God") was the outcome of the very private resurrection in the tomb, hidden behind a sealed door, upon the cherubim-flanked "lid of the Ark."

James Jordan speaks about the Ark as God's treasure chest, locked up until the coming of the Messiah. It contained Word, Sacrament and Government. When the Jews chose Barabbas over Jesus, they unwittingly opened the Ark, and blood and water flowed out. They exposed themselves to the realities behind the Old Covenant curses and blessings. They also spilled out the hidden treasures of wisdom and knowledge for the life of the whole world.

In the Book of Kings, the account of the Temple's construction follows the feasts pattern, and the blood on the olivewood doors is the finest gold. Passover is about doors being *covered*. Atonement is about doors being *opened*. The golden doors are opened towards the end of the ceremony and the Shekinah glory fills the house.

No one but the priests were allowed to see inside the Tabernacle, or even to see the furniture when it was on the move. But they all knew what went on in there! The true religion is not a mystery religion. Many things are private, but there are no "secret rites." There are no Masons or Mormons in the true faith. The privacy is the wisdom of the head, and what goes on in there always flows out into the world, whether it be answers to prayer, edifying legislation, godly offspring, or a righteous nation.

Men are structure (Word – singular); women are glory (Government – plural). A man's glory is secret. A woman's glory, in every way, is public. A husband is glorified by the smile—or exposed by the scowl or black eye—on his wife.

A pregnant belly is a glory or a shame depending on the man. (A friend of mine once said the reason she never had children was she had never met a man she wanted to reproduce!)

Sometimes the revelation of what has gone on in secret is a sudden one. When a crisis comes, even in an unforeseen irritation, our inward lack of faith and peace is exposed in half a second of rage, like a naptha flash, and burned forever into someone's retinas. Are we those whose years of secret sin can be suddenly exposed in a swift and very public fall? Will the adult lives of our children be a public testimony to a lack of tenderness and guidance in the privacy of the home? Or will we be those whose years of godly self-discipline and self-sacrifice will be abruptly allowed to shine when the crisis comes? Doctor Jesus' X-rays can be a midlife crisis or a call to martyrdom.

For churches, the end of a denomination can come suddenly, but only after years of inward compromise. God always gets an Ezekiel to dig through the wall. What will the son of man find we have been constructing when the harsh light is allowed in? The day will always declare it.

A bankrupt business or global financial crisis also issues from the secret places. Even secret abortions leave their mark on an individual, and then on a culture. Word becomes deed. Sex begets seed. Fruit is inescapable, even if that "fruit" is barrenness.

Bob Jones, Sr. said, "Back of every tragedy in human

character is a slow process of wicked thinking." I've seen this in my life. Thank God for the washing of the water of the Word.

What goes on in secret always ends up shouted from the housetops—unless of course there is blood on the door already, in which case your household is passed over when the destroyer comes and the firstborn "issues forth" alive in the morning. The Herodian "man of sin" Temple was a stillborn. The son of man, *totus Christus,* now has family all over the world.

The Bible contains many "hidden things," but there are no eternal mysteries. Every veil will be torn. The tree of wisdom is only hidden from us until we are ready. After a long betrothal, water suddenly becomes wine.

It seems the Lord isn't that good at keeping secrets. In hindsight, we can see that throughout the Old Testament there were many things the Lord was busting to tell us that we weren't ready for. So He just prefigured them a thousand times to get us ready for the One who called Himself the Open Door.

He calls us not merely to salvation, but to wise government from the secret places, the places from where new life issues like pure water from the creative Word.

> *Keep your heart with all vigilance,*
> *for from it flow the springs of life.*
> (Proverbs 4:23)

Baptism and the Lord's table come from the body of Jesus. Fasting is a sacrament we can give from our *own* bodies...

12

Fasting as sacrament

FEEDING THE WHITE DOG

As discussed in the previous chapter, living things have brains, guts and outsides. This is Word, Sacrament and Government.

So, basically, as a Tabernacle, if my mind is a symbol of the command from the Most Holy (Word), and my arms and legs carry out my thoughts and intents in the world (Government), what is in between? The Holy Place, the place of flesh offered to God.

The human heart is desperately wicked and deceitful (Jeremiah 17:9). The fallen mind is the Most Unholy. What comes out of it is what makes us unclean, not what goes in (Mark 7:20). It is the mind that makes the flesh unholy.

But as Christians, we also have the mind of Christ. There is a black dog and a white dog. As one of my pastors used to say, whichever dog you feed the most will become the strongest. That's true. But we are to *kill* the black dog.

Fasting is a form of death in the flesh. It is a temporary refusal of the Covenant blessings for the sake of those outside the Covenant. It is becoming "accursed" that we may win our brothers (Romans 9:3). Blood opens the door for the mind of Christ (the true Ark) and mortifies the lawless mind of Adam.[1] It is a refusal of the Tree of Judicial Wisdom until we ourselves are judged in the stead of another.

When we fast, we become broken bread and poured out wine. It is not a sacrament received, like baptism and the Lord's table. These come from the body of Jesus. Fasting is a sacrament we can give from our *own* bodies for greater kingdom government. And a greater kingdom means a greater feast when we are done. Fasting gives us somebody new to eat *with*. We are Adam with his guts emptied to build Greater Eve.

Like Jesus, we are "torn in two" under the Covenant curse, that we may be put back together in greater glory, bread and wine reunited at Solomon's wedding feast.

---

1   Both Zechariah 5 and Revelation 20 show the true Ark lid being opened and the false ark bound under a heavy lid and exiled. In both cases it was by the blood of Atonement. Fasting casts the Wickedness-woman, and the man of lawlessness, into outer darkness. In Revelation, it was the massacre of the saints as bread and wine in chapter 14 that provided the first goat. But that's another story.

Do not deprive one another, except perhaps by agreement for a limited time, that you may devote yourselves to prayer; but then come together again, so that Satan may not tempt you because of your lack of self-control. (1 Corinthians 7:5)

The Most Holy Place was unseen by all except the High Priest. It pictured the tomb of Christ, and it was not a doorway to another world but a doorway to *this* world transformed, renewed.

Likewise, the Holy Place was unseen by all except the priesthood. With the mind of Christ, we enter into Christ's ministry in this secondary domain. Fasting in the hidden place allows God to bless—to vindicate—our ministry with very public rewards (Matthew 6:17).

Fasting makes one into food, a living sacrifice, a mediator between a world starving for God and the unimaginable feast He has planned for a righteous humanity.

Fasting is a taste of death

"Fasting is a way of entering death, for
if you don't get food, you will die.
One enters death in the hope of
resurrection."

— James B. Jordan, *Mordecai Plays Politics (Esther 4)*,
Biblical Horizons N° 228.

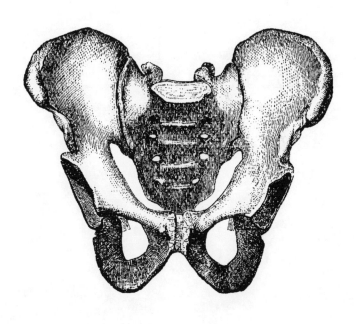

Unlike Adam, Jacob realized that every serpentine challenge came from the hand of God. He crushed them through crafty obedience and gained great wisdom.

13

Jacob's hollow

WRESTLING WITH GOD IN THE FLESH

Whoever among the sons of Aaron offers the blood of the peace offerings and the fat shall have the right thigh for a portion. (Leviticus 7:33)

NATURALISTS BELIEVE THAT THE SIMILARITIES between animals and humans indicate common ancestry. Creation scientists tell us that they indicate a common Creator.

But there is more. James Jordan believes that animals are like an earthly class of angels, servants from God to teach us things. He notes that animals find water, avoid poisonous plants and sense danger before humans do. Different species also illustrate various facets of the human and Divine personalities, hence the wide use of animals in children's books. The "animal kingdoms" of the Old Testament were a time of childhood.

Like God's throne, Adam's throne was surrounded by beasts. Though Adam was not part of the animal kingdom, he shared the same breath and represented that kingdom before God. An angel-animal hybrid[1] was the first false teacher, the first lying prophet in the king's court. When Adam sinned, his entire kingdom suffered. Judgment came upon all flesh.

Man represented the animals. When the sentence of death was executed, in God's mercy, animals represented Man. But Adam and Eve also wore the skins of the sacrifices. Adam again represented the animals. They became his glory and he became their life. We see this process again in Noah and finally in Christ. This is the "world" of the Bible, a place where identity, mediation and representation are communicated in physical ways, and it is the world in which we live.

When the Apostle Paul uses the term "flesh," he speaks within that same world. He speaks symbolically only because flesh itself is symbolic, a *type* of something else.

Even in death, the animals teach us. Fleshly animals were blameless substitutes for sinful, fleshly men. When the books of Moses give detailed instructions concerning the head, skin, flesh, offal, fat and legs of the sacrificial animals, they suggest to us the typological significance of the bodily functions within our own "temples."

1 The serpent was perhaps the first union of heaven and earth, a false Shekinah, a king composed "before God's time."

GOD (WORD)

MAN IMAGES GOD (SACRAMENT)

ANIMALS SUBMIT TO MAN (GOVERNMENT)

The Word became flesh, in Adam and in Jesus, so the "anatomical worship" carried out with animals is not only a substitutionary judgment upon Adam and the nations. The careful details are an exposition of the nature of God as revealed in the structure of Man. The Bible's common use of words such as "bowels" and "reins," mostly replaced in modern translations, is perhaps not primitive idiom but language intended to lead us back, via a "biblical homology," to the inner workings of the Trinity. James Jordan writes:

> ...it is the "fat" of the sacrifice that is considered God's food, and thus turned into smoke for Him to inhale— the sacrificial equivalent of eating. This is not just any fat on the animal, but the fat of the inward parts, given in Leviticus 3:3-4 as "the fat that covers the inner parts and all the fat that is on the inner parts, and the two kidneys with the fat that is on them, which is on the loins, and the lobe of the liver, which he shall remove with the kidneys" (cf. vv. 9-10, 14-15). The summary of these verses is that "all fat is the Lord's. It is a perpetual statute throughout your generations in all your dwellings: You shall not eat any fat or any blood" (vv. 16-17).

What emerges from this is that "fat" includes the kidneys and the liver, as well as the fat around them. "Fat" thus correlates to "inward parts." The kidneys, claimed by God, are part of a man's inward being. They are tested by God (Psalm 7:9; Jeremiah 11:20, 17:10). They instruct or convict a man (Psalms 16:7; 73:21). But most importantly, God possesses the kidneys (or reins) of the righteous (Psalm 139:13). The word translated here as "loins" also denotes the inward parts of a man (Psalm 38:7), and the liver is also used for the inner man (Proverbs 7:23; Lamentations 2:11).

It is the inward parts that belong to God. Only God knows the heart. Only God tests the kidneys. As the Lord reminded Samuel, "God sees not as man sees, for man looks at the appearance, but the Lord looks at the heart" (1 Samuel 16:7). It is forbidden for a man to try and take possession of the inward parts of another man, whether through cannibalism or brainwashing or any other means. The rule of man over man is to be limited only to the externals of life. In the kingdom of God, the inner man is sacrificed and taken into the life of God though the outer man perishes until the day of resurrection.[2]

The "inner workings" of God are expressed in the architecture of Man, and the "inner workings" of the Temple signify this to us. The "anatomical worship" described to

2   James B. Jordan, *Studies in Food and Faith,* "The Meaning of Eating in the Bible."

Moses was humanity observing the work of the Great Physician: not the flesh-to-flesh process of surgery, but the transformation of each part of the body, and its God-given role, into the image of God—by *consumption.*

This *"Genetic"* background explains Israel's refusal to consume the corresponding part of the bodies of animals after God's crippling of Jacob in Genesis 32. Jordan writes:

> Jacob had wrestled with Esau all his life. He had wrestled with his father all his adult life. He had wrestled with Laban for twenty years. It could have been any of these three who attacked him that night but it wasn't. It was God with whom Jacob had to do.
>
> As the dawn began to break, the person with whom Jacob wrestled "touched the socket of his thigh; so the socket of Jacob's thigh was dislocated while he wrestled with him" (Genesis 32:25). Jacob then realized that he had been wrestling with God. God—the Angel of Yahweh—said "Let me go, for the dawn is breaking," but Jacob refused to let go until he had been blessed. So God said, "Your name shall no longer be Jacob [One Who Supplants Another (by wrestling)]; but Israel [One Who Strives With God (by wrestling)]; for you have striven [as Israel] with God and [as Jacob] with men, and you have prevailed" (Genesis 32:28).[3]

---

3   James B. Jordan, *Primeval Saints: Studies in the Patriarchs of Genesis,* p. 111.

Jacob's life of wrestling was not a punishment from God. It was intended to make him strong. But what was the architectural significance of the *location* of the wound?

The relationship between Jacob and the animals, and later the Aaronic High Priest and the nation of Israel, was a type of that between Israel and the nations. Israel was the ceremonially clean sacrificial "head," and the nations were the bridal "body".

Jacob's journey to and from Haran follows the Bible Matrix, which echoes the sacrificial *"totus Christus."* On his way to Haran, Jacob's *head* rested upon an unhewn stone, symbolizing an altar. He was carrying the Adamic curse of a barren Land. On his return, it was his *body* that was offered. The dismembered legs of the sacrifice were washed and offered to complete the process. The curse here must be "Evian." The lower parts of the body have to do with offspring. Jacob, as the "bridal man," was carrying the curse upon Greater Eve. He had to be wounded before he rejoined his father's house.

Perhaps the clue here is the word "thigh." Generational Covenant blessings involved the one being blessed putting his hand "under the thigh" of the one doing the blessing. Some believe this involved the younger touching the testicles of the elder. The proven fruitfulness of the father was being transferred to, identified with, the son. The word "thigh" also relates to the fruitfulness of females:

And when he has made her drink the water, then, if she has defiled herself and has broken faith with her husband, the water that brings the curse shall enter into her and cause bitter pain, and her womb shall swell, and her thigh shall fall away, and the woman shall become a curse among her people. (Numbers 5:27)

So, Jacob's brow and thigh were offered to God, and he was invested as a prince. Unlike Adam, Jacob realized that every serpentine challenge came from the hand of God. He crushed them through crafty obedience and gained great wisdom. His wound, like the wounds of Jesus, the Lamb of God, would be borne in his body as a memorial. For now, Jacob was the offspring of the Woman.

This might also explain Jacob's generosity towards Esau. Jacob had fled into the wilderness (as Head), empty, alone, and without a place to lay his head. He was now returning "full" as a new house (with Body), a sheltering tent. He knew that the abundance—wives, servants and animals— was from God's hand and was a glory not to be coveted.

Moreover, we have the significance of the two pillars of Solomon's Temple—the "legs" of the house—as two brothers, priest and king, Jew and Gentile. On his way out, Jacob saw the "ziggurat" House of God in a dream.[4]

---

4   The pillars, Jachin and Boaz, represent the Creation process of forming and filling: establishment (a priestly foundation) and strength (kingly rule). For a full explanation of the significance of the architecture of Jacob's dream, see James B. Jordan, *Through New Eyes*, pp. 87-89.

Upon his return, he himself was blessed as the prefigurement of that House *in flesh*—a human Temple mediating between God and men.

Fighting sin and resting in Christ are two edges of the same blade.

14

Joints and marrow

For the word of God is living and active, sharper than any two-edged sword, piercing to the division of [breath] and of spirit, of joints and of marrow, and discerning the thoughts and intentions of the heart. (Hebrews 4:12)

FOR MANY YEARS I THOUGHT THE PHRASE "joints and marrow" in this verse was very strange. I guess this is a testimony to the artificial division by most Bible teachers of Old and New Testament thought. It refers to the sword of the priest cutting up the sacrifice.

The division begins in Genesis 1. God divides three times to make three empty spaces. Then God divides Adam to construct Eve.

At the beginning of the year, Passover involves division, both of the sacrificial yearling (lamb or goat) and of the Hebrews from the Egyptians. Matching this chiastically is the division between the two goats at Atonement, towards the end of the year. One goes to heaven, the other goes to hell. How might this apply to the Christian?

Fighting sin and resting in Christ are two edges of the

same blade. We are commanded to do both. The Lord said He had given the Land and its enemies into Joshua's hand, but there were still battles to fight. It is the fighting that brings maturity. Even Christ had to fight sin to become mature (perfect).

All the way through the Bible, God gives a man a mission, tests him, and then assesses him (judgment). This judgment is always a "Day of Coverings" where one goat goes to heaven and the other goes to hell. The disciples stay with Jesus in the upper room but Judas is sent to destruction.

As individuals, each of us will be finally divided in two under the Covenant curse. The bad is sent to destruction and the redeemed ascends to God clothed in glorious flames, covered by the blood of our High Priest that was presented first.

But the division begins now—as we are divided like a sacrifice, to joints and marrow—by God's Word. Bad you is already dying, and you are to mortify him all the more. Despair over your sin is a work of the Spirit. But so is the sure hope of final redemption. In Hebrew, Avenger and Redeemer are the same word.

Like Christ, we are all "torn in two" under the Covenant. Each one is a veil of flesh and the final tearing is a door. The context of Hebrews 4:12 is, after all, *rest.*

Food for God

"Human beings were not acceptable food for God in the Old Covenant, because of sin. Accordingly, they were excluded from His full presence, the Holy of Holies. In the Mosaic system, however, Israelites were permitted to offer themselves as food for God by means of substitutes. Only with the coming of Jesus Christ was a man found who was acceptable 'food' for God, and only Jesus was permitted to enter fully into God's presence (Rev. 4-5). In union with Him, of course, we all have this privilege. God smells Jesus in us, and we taste like Him, because we have been united to Him and because we have 'eaten His flesh and drunk His blood': and so, God is pleased to 'eat' us into His full presence."

— James B. Jordan, *Studies in Food and Faith*

It was the bloody rock of priesthood that gave Jesus the keys to death and Sheol to set the captives free.

15

Upon this rock

And the angel of God said unto him, Take the flesh and the unleavened cakes, and lay them upon this rock, and pour out the broth. And he did so. (Judges 6:20 KJV)

And I say also unto thee, That thou art Peter, and upon this rock I will build my church; and the gates of hell shall not prevail against it. (Matthew 16:18 KJV)

As MUCH AS IT DISTRESSES US AND MAKES US FLINCH, the cross is central to the process of building the Church. The heavenly city is always founded on blood, on a rough cut altar stone like Jacob's pillow. It is a rock anointed with oil and blood and fire, a miniature Sinai. It smashed the political kingdoms of the Gentiles to pieces and is now filling the earth. The Land is always purified with blood. The kingdom is only ever bought with blood.

GOD'S KITCHEN

THE GATES OF HELL

The gate of the city is where judgment takes place. The bars of Sheol (Jonah 2) keep the captives under lock and key, and justly so. Satan is a liar, but his accusations are based on truth. It was the bloody rock of priesthood that gave Jesus the keys to death and Sheol to set the captives free. A white stone gave Him the key to the bottomless pit to bind the strong man and spoil his vessels.[1]

THE KEY TO THE KINGDOM

And now He offers to us that same key. It is a rock upon which one may lay one's head at the foundations of the city. The blood goes up and the Spirit comes down. When the body of flesh is broken and the broth poured out and the jars of clay are shattered, the flaming eyes of Pentecost surround the enemy. The adversary is blinded, his troops slaughter each other in the confusion, and the people of God are freed. But the slaughter begins at a lonely rock.

The foundation of any church is a blood-covered rock, an altar stone with a head offered willingly upon it. If the Midianites, Amalekites, Herodians and Romans are still running the show, it is because the rock is dry.

---

1   If a white stone was drawn from the ephod on the Day of Atonement, the sins of Israel were covered. The same process was used in the time of Ezra to identify those who were acceptable to God as priests after their genealogies had been lost. Jesus offers the white stone of martyrdom to the saints of Pergamos in Revelation 2.

True apostolic succession is a willingness to be a living sacrifice.

16

Binding and loosing

No one can enter a strong man's house and plunder his goods, unless he first binds the strong man. And then he will plunder his house. (Mark 3:27 NKJV)

MUCH COMMENTARY ON THE REVELATION seems oblivious to its allusions to the Pentateuch (although there are many that do enlighten us concerning many isolated points). Even the "binding" of Satan in Revelation has an Old Testament background.

This act by Jesus has a "sacrificial" element, and it is only half the process. The process we observe throughout the Bible is one of binding and loosing. The "head" is bound that the "body" might be loosed. A husband is bound to one wife that she might have freedom to shine in a safe domain. Adam was bound under a single Law that Eve might not be deceived. Abram was "bound" by circumcision that Sarai's womb might be "freed." The bondwoman and her son were cast out that the son of the freewoman might be the heir. Isaac was quite literally bound that Israel's *tribal* future might be freed. Joseph was bound that Israel's *national* future might be freed. Animals were sacrificed so Israel could be redeemed. Israel was bound under Moses for the sake of the nations, but they "broke loose" with the golden calf.

We also see a hint of this process in Daniel 3:

> Then King Nebuchadnezzar was astonished and rose up in haste. He declared to his counselors, "Did we not cast three men bound into the fire?" They answered and said to the king, "True, O king." He answered and said, "But I see four men unbound, walking in the midst of the fire, and they are not hurt; and the appearance of the fourth is like a son of the gods." (Daniel 3:24-25)

Moving to the New Testament, Jesus was bound by soldiers so that the disciples might be freed. At the Lord's Table, the past was bound and broken in Jesus, and the future was released, poured out as new wine.

Then, the apostles were bound that the Gentiles might be freed. This willing submission of the apostles to being "bound" for the hope of Israel (Acts 28:20) is what resulted in AD70, and the binding of Satan. That is what their faithful witness achieved.

> Most assuredly, I say to you, when you were younger, you girded yourself and walked where you wished; but when you are old, you will stretch out your hands, and

another will gird you and carry you where you do not wish. (John 21:18 NKJV)

True apostolic succession is a willingness to be a living sacrifice. As followers of Christ, we are bound (in prayer and fasting) that others might be freed. The idea is that Satan is bound with us, we take him to the altar (or grave, or furnace) and leave him there, while we ourselves are freed, "resurrected" along with his captives. It is the ministry of Christ in miniature.

The application in Revelation might be complicated, but the process isn't. The Revelation, indeed all the New Testament, must be expounded with reference to the processes founded in the Torah.

The fall of Jerusalem in AD70 was the Lord's Table played out on an imperial scale. Satan was bound in AD70 that the nations might be freed. The Lord's Table, and its representatives, mediate between heaven and earth.

I will give you the keys of the kingdom of heaven, and whatever you bind on earth shall be bound in heaven, and whatever you loose on earth shall be loosed in heaven. (Matthew 16:19)

Someone carries the curse so that history can move on freely. Someone is bound so that somebody else may be loosed.

17

Silence of
the Lamb

*When he had spoken to me according to these words, I
turned my face toward the ground and was mute.*
(Daniel 10:15)

THE DOMINION PATTERN ALWAYS BEGINS with a Word from
God. The one to whom He speaks experiences a "Passover,"
a purifying, symbolic death-and-resurrection. The new
prophet is then "raised" to his feet (as Firstfruits) and
given a task. Filled with God's Word, he opens it to the
intended audience (Pentecost).[1]

The one who falls then rises is the mediator of a new
covenant. Adam sleeps so he can be married to Eve.
Abram sleeps so his "belly" can fill the world with living
waters. The prophets fall as dead men before the chariot-

---

1   Notice this pattern in the structure of Revelation. The *Firstfruits* Lamb
    opens the scroll; the scroll culminates in coals from the heavenly altar
    (Pentecost) which begins the *Trumpets* of warning: the witness of the
    apostles, men with purifying fire coming from their mouths.

throne of God so their words can slay the old order and initiate a new one.

> On that day your mouth will be opened to the fugitive, and you shall speak and be no longer mute. So you will be a sign to them, and they will know that I am the Lord. (Ezekiel 24:27)

In Luke 1, after the Word from God, it is Zechariah's unbelief that makes him dumb. He himself becomes a silent Passover lamb, a sign to an Israel that has become a new Egypt. In the silence, sacrificial blood is applied so that history may continue. A man falls (Zechariah) so that another may rise (John).

Zechariah was made dumb so that John could speak. In the same way, Lot's wife was "sterilized" at the same time that Sarah conceived; Saul received an evil spirit when David received the Holy Spirit. Someone carries the curse so that history may move on freely. Someone is bound so that somebody else may be loosed.

Sin crouches at the door, so that is where the covering blood of silent obedience is shed. Somebody provides cover so the people of God can be free. Somebody falls into the ground as seed and dies. Someone always takes "The Fall."

When, centuries earlier, the prophet Zechariah saw a vision in the Temple, it was of Satan attempting to prevent the reinstitution (or re-*covering*) of the Aaronic priest-hood after the captivity. The Accuser stood at God's right hand—at Zechariah's left—the Lampstand as the Law-eyes of God. The angel of the Lord presumably stood at Zechariah's right—the Table of Showbread.

The devil occupied the place he usurped from Adam. Adam would take the throne from him via sacrifice, and a new priesthood would be made clean. Man only becomes a lucifer, a light-bearer, via the Table of bread and wine. (The governing lights of Day 4 always come after the new grain and fruit of Day 3.)

After the High Priest was reclothed, Prophet Zechariah saw a Lampstand. Instead of the usual seven it had forty-nine lights, an abundance of Spirit glory in God's people.

But in the New Testament, the angel promised a child, John, who would be filled with "Pentecost" from birth, a walking Lampstand, a burning bush proclaiming a new Exodus.

From the angel, Priest Zechariah took the place of the Table (silence—divided by the Word) so that John could speak as a Lampstand, proclaiming the *Ethics* of a New Covenant.

There is always a Passover Lamb before the Pentecost, always half an hour of silence before the seven thunders, always a willing Altar before the Coals of Fire glorify the sacrifice. And after the silence comes the song.

When Priest Zechariah spoke again, it was after he wrote concerning the miraculous son at his right hand, "His name is 'the Lord is gracious'." His mouth was opened for the first time in the best part of a year.

God's mouth too was opened for the first time in 400 years. A new nation was ready to be born out of the corpse of Egypt.

But, like his father, John's mouth would also be silenced so that history could continue in the Lamb to which they all pointed. This Lamb Himself would be silenced for the sake of a Pentecostal witness—a declaration of vengeance and redemption—to the world.

There is good silence and there is bad silence. We listen obediently to God that we may speak for God.

The half-hour of silence

"This is how long the saints have to wait before God begins His avenging of them. The continuous singing of the angels ceases while the trumpets blow, so that they can be heard. The trumpets last for a half-hour. The trumpets last from Pentecost to the harvest of the Firstfruits Church just before AD70."

— James B. Jordan, *The Seven Seals of Revelation,*
Biblical Horizons Nº 72.

God's creative process is sacrificial. He is a *butcher* who tears things apart. It is also culinary. He is a *chef* who puts things together in new ways.

18

Creation and Communion

PRETERISTS AND THE LORD'S SUPPER

For as often as you eat this bread and drink the cup, you proclaim the Lord's death until he comes.
(1 Corinthians 11:26)

IF, AS PRETERISTS MAINTAIN, the imminent "coming" of Jesus occurred in AD70, why do we still celebrate the Lord's Supper?

To answer as an "orthodox" preterist (one who maintains that there is yet a future resurrection and judgment), I would mention that Communion is a Covenant memorial that reminds *God* of the Covenant. The *Covenant* is the key.

At His ascension, Jesus opened a new scroll (Revelation 4-5), the *New* Covenant. In AD70, he rolled up the *Old* Covenant, the one that was like an old garment, ready to pass away. There was a forty year "wilderness" overlap

135

from the beginning of the new era to the end of the old. The idea of an open scroll or a garment aligns the Covenant with the firmament. It is a mediatory covering, a veil which shields us from direct exposure, being face to face with, the Law of God.

Those who refused to take shelter under the New Covenant during this 40 year "generation" were left "uncovered" when it was ended. They cried "Cover us!" as Jesus predicted. But only the saints were covered—the Firstfruits Church.

Well, that deals with those who kept breaking bread as Jesus commanded until His coming. Where does that leave every Christian and church since AD70? First, we must understand the symbolic, "Creational," process of Communion.

God's creative process is sacrificial. He is a butcher who tears things apart. It is also culinary. He is a chef who puts things together in new ways. God always *divides, fills* and *reunites.* In Communion, the bread and wine must be offered separately—"divided." As the sacrifice, Christ's body was divided from His blood. We are filled, and His body and blood are reunited—put back together again— in us. As we partake, we fulfill His resurrection as His body, a holy army (Ezekiel 37; John 12:24).

In the two trees, Life and Wisdom, bread and wine, priest and king, flesh and blood, Land and Sea, earth and heaven, the Lord presented Adam with a divided world. The only way it could be united was through obedience. If he obeyed the Father's will, he would eat the bread, then drink the wine, and the divided world would be united first *in his own body*. This is what Christ accomplished in His resurrection in the Garden (as a new Eden).

The triune theme of Garden, Land, World recurs throughout the Bible.[1] Christ conquered in the Garden. The Church conquered in the Land and AD70 finished the Jew-Gentile divide begun in Abraham. But there is still work to do, so we are given the last supper elements separately. As His body, we are one, but the World which God has given us to subdue for Him is not. Dominion begins liturgically with bread and wine as separate elements, united in our bodies, renewing the Covenant weekly until the entire World is a Holy Place.

"If the marriage feast was in AD70, why do we still take Communion?" Christ's coming in AD70 finished the union of Jew and Gentile. But there is a greater feast to come at the second resurrection when the work is complete. Then Christ, victorious over Garden (Adam: Most Holy Place), Land (Cain: Holy Place) and World (Sons of God: Gentile Courts) will present the kingdom to

---

1 For more discussion on this subject, see James Jordan's *Through New Eyes* and Peter Leithart's *A House for My Name*.

the Father, the entire creation as a new Tabernacle.

Christ came in judgment at the end of the Old Covenant. He will also come in judgment at the completion of the New Covenant. That is the nature of Covenants, and this is the future coming we look forward to when we celebrate as faithful "sons of God" in the World.

Preterists celebrate the Lord's supper because AD70 was not the *culmination* of the New Covenant era but the *inauguration.*

Eating with God

"There were no sacrificial meals until the Exodus. The patriarchs before Noah, those after the Flood, and the Hebrew patriarchs offered whole burnt sacrifices, but they never ate any portion of them. It was a distinct benefit and advantage of the Mosaic economy that God pitched His tent in the midst of Israel and set up a system whereby they might eat at His house with Him. Once the Tabernacle was set up, all kinds of boundary rules and laws of cleanness came into being as a result. Among them was the restriction of holy food only to the priests."

— James B. Jordan, *Studies in Food and Faith.*

As a "human shield,"
a firmament of flesh,
the office of Mediator
is a position of
passivity towards
God, and *activity*
towards Creation.

19

Deus ex machina

COVENANT AS HUMAN SHIELD

---

*But woe to you, scribes and Pharisees, hypocrites! For you
shut the kingdom of heaven in [men's] faces. For you neither
enter yourselves nor allow those who would enter to go in.*
(Matthew 23:13)

ALL CREATION IS COVENANTAL, AND THEREFORE all relationships within it have a hierarchical structure. God calls a
vassal *(Creation)*, separates/sanctifies him as a delegated
authority *(Division)*. He gives him a job to do *(Ascension)*,
and a period of time to accomplish it.

This Adam, the Covenant Mediator, stands between
heaven and earth (Land). The Land was raised out of the
Sea, and the Man was raised out of the Land as "grain and
fruit." Then this new house, this body of broken earth,
was filled with heaven, with the Spirit of God, sun moon
and stars: This Adam was to be a singular prism which
would expand the white light of God into plural lights, a

greater body, the full spectrum of color. But he was to be a broken man. The light had to pass *through* him.

The passed-through man is a preacher who is *given* the Word, *opens* the Word, and *explains* the Word. The pulpit is the place of Adam lifted up, a man of grain and fruit made by the Spirit into broken bread and poured-out wine. When he breaks the bread, Jesus is recognized in him, and the people become a united, self-governing body.

As a "human shield," a firmament of flesh, the office of Mediator is a position of *passivity* towards God, and *activity* towards Creation. Willing slavery to God brings dominion over the world. When Adam refuses to be bread and wine (a slave to the will of the Father), he makes slaves of those he was supposed to lead by his sacrificial example. They become his food, and he becomes bars and gates instead of The Door. When his children, his parish, his employees look up for light, the heaven is brass. An abdication of personal slavery to Christ does not bring an egalitarian utopia. The good yoke of Covenant hierarchy cannot be broken, only perverted into a burden for those it was supposed to shield and shelter. If obedience is shirked, the burden is multiplied (like offspring) and borne by the body. When the perversion is full-grown, God sends a sword and makes a New Covenant.

Slavery in the Bible is a hot topic, and James Jordan observes that it cannot be properly understood without the biblical understanding of man's relationships to God, to fellow man, and to the sub-human creation. He writes:

Man's foundational relationship with God is one of total *passivity.* God is wholly—radically and comprehensively—Lord, and man is wholly slave...

The Bible also reveals that man is the image and likeness of God and that he has been given dominion over the sub-human creation, and especially over the animals (Gen. 1:26-28; 2:19-20). Thus, man's preeminent relationship with the sub-human creation is one of *activity:* Man is Lord, and the sub-human creations are slaves of man. Man's lordship over the sub-human creation is, however, not absolute, for man is not the Creator of the sub-human creation. Rather, man's lordship is relative to God's primary mastery, and is under His Law...

The Bible further reveals that all men are descended from Adam the first man, and are of one blood. Thus, all men have the same essential ontological status. Whatever differences in abilities, age, and sex may appear in humanity, there is an essential or foundational equality among all men. Man's relationship with his fellowman is, then, essentially one of mutuality, reciprocity, or coequality.

It emerges that man has relationships with three spheres of existence: God, the sub-human creation, and fellowman. It follows that man's nature is in part defined in terms of these three relationships and that man has a need rightly to be related to each of these three spheres. A complex of right relations is a situation of order; the rebellion of man, however, introduced a situation of disorder. Man's rebellion against God entailed a perversion of all relationships, but not an effacement of man's nature. Man, being author neither of his own existence nor of his own essence, can destroy neither. He is still essentially a creature who needs an absolute reference point, a supreme master, to whom he can relate with absolute passivity. Man's rejection of the Creator as God does not result in his having no god at all, but in his having some false god. Man does not obliterate his psychological need for an absolute, he "exchanges" it for a lie (Romans 1:23). Thus, man may be said to have a "slave drive" which ever seeks some god to submit to...

Just as man does not cease to be a slave when he rebels against God, neither does he cease to be "dominion man". Rather, his "dominical drive" is simply redirected and perverted. Nor does man cease to be a being who needs relationships of mutuality with equals. He remains a social being. Man can no more eliminate his essence than he can his existence, for both are authored not by himself, but by God.[1]

Just as the obedience of one man becomes institutionalized (i.e. it takes on a body), so does the disobedience. Adam's sin multiplied into that of Cain; Cain's multiplied

1   James B. Jordan, *Slavery in Biblical Perspective*, 1980.

into that of Lamech, and Lamech's violence, once amplified, ended the world. Offspring amplifies. The sins with which Gideon toys are fully embraced by Abimelech.

In Revelation, John wept because the end of the world was nigh. The Old Covenant had failed and judgment was at hand. There was no one, in heaven, on the Land, or under the Land (in the Gentile "Sea"), who was able to stand in the gap. He describes the heavenly realities of all the Tabernacle furnitures except for one crucial piece, the Table of Bread and Wine. Creation, History and Covenant were apparently at an end—until John spied the standing Lamb.

How could the disastrous first century situation of a priesthood bound by personal, communal and state slavery (under the Herods as the "face" of Rome) be reversed by the obedience of a single Man? And then how could this reversal spread so quickly over a few centuries to encompass the known world? Was it a *deus ex machina* cop-out rescue after the truly impossible cliffhanger? No. God is a better screenwriter than that. In all the best stories, the surprise of salvation is all the more satisfying because its credibility rests upon something innate, or even hidden, in the original premise.

The Old Testament is not merely a trail of clues left by a divine Agatha Christie, clues that only make sense when the denouement finally arrives (although that's how most moderns teach the Bible!). The Old Testament is a search for a faithful Covenant head to replace Adam, beginning with Cain and Abel. Certainly, they are types of the Christ, but the Covenants these men were to keep were real enough.

So, Christ could reverse the trajectory of all humanity by being lifted up as bread and wine in the Covenant "machine." One Man as Head can make a door that many can pass through as Body, whether he be a husband, a father, an employer, a minister, a president, or Christ Himself, our Human Shield.

That is the heart of Covenant: *passivity* towards God (death) and *activity* towards Creation (resurrection), with *equality* towards fellow man—brotherhood—in between. If one of these is missing we are left with either impotent pietism, tyranny or violent revolution. This place of tension, this seemingly impossible position, is where Adam's dominion, Christ's kingdom, is found. It is the paradox of a living sacrifice.

Covenant is a choice between God's device and the gods of our own devising. It is the difference between Abel and Cain, between blessing and cursing. Both are slavery, but we are invited to choose our Master.

A satisfied intellect

The theory of evolution allows
Richard Dawkins to be an
"intellectually satisfied atheist."
The universe *has* no purpose, but man
can purpose. Thus, man is god.

But then, what purpose is there
in intellectual satiety? Our
self-consciousness and curiosity
have only led us into trouble.
A satisfied brain is less important,
Darwinianly-speaking, than a full belly.

One might object that, in our modern
world, a full brain is required for a full
belly. But if we really are just nature's
way of keeping meat fresh, a full brain
tastes the same as an empty one.

The societal fruits of the great revivals were exactly the kinds of things the (non-revivalist) proponents of dominion theology crave to see in our time.

20

Revivals and farming

And let us not grow weary of doing good, for in due season we will reap, if we do not give up. (Galatians 6:9)

IN 1976, J. EDWIN ORR GAVE A SERMON in which he summarized his work on the history of revivals. His main point was that revivals all began with unified, cross-denominational prayer. Recorded on film for posterity, it is a very friendly yet stunning address.

Revivalism cops heat from mainline denominations, and often for good reason. But the societal fruits of the historical events which Orr shared were exactly the kinds of things the proponents of dominion theology crave to see in our time. And they happened *overnight.* What's the deal?

The clue is farming. Many Australians remember Billy Graham's "windfall" in 1959, an event during which many of those who initially tried to prevent the rallies and then heckled them suddenly came to know Christ. But when Graham returned in the 70s, the results were not as bountiful. What made the difference? A combination of fewer children in Sunday School and a greater commitment to Naturalism in public education.

What dominion theologians get right is long-term planning, planting, watering, discipleship. They are masters of the plod-in-the-sod. What the revivalists get right is harvest time, and they look for and pray for the unusual working of the Spirit.

The dominionists need to differentiate between the true harvest when it comes, and the Satanic counterfeits that always follow—the revivalist excesses which they rightly fear. The revivalists need to stop pining for harvest, or manufacturing fake ones, and keep about the patient business of preaching and discipleship. Kingdom *will* come when it is ready.

Unified prayer is not a "red button" labeled REVIVAL which God waits for us to press. Certainly, we should be praying, and unified. But Orr made the point that before the great revivals, when things were in many ways worse than they are now, *God Himself* moved certain men to pray. He called them into His presence as human channels for what was coming anyway, just as He does in the Bible.

Harvest time comes when the Husbandman is ready. He brings the increase. We can neither force His hand nor stop that sickle when He starts swinging it.

Evangelical whack-a-mole

"I don't want us to be playing evangelical whack-a-mole. The earthier aspects of the Reformed faith were whacked for the sake of revivalism. But if we whack 'revivalism,' and begin to neglect preaching for true and abiding conversion, then we are just going to rebuild the kind of cobwebby Christendom that the next Kierkegaard will have a ball making fun of."

— Douglas Wilson,
A Huge Mountain Range of Cotton Candy,
www.dougwils.com

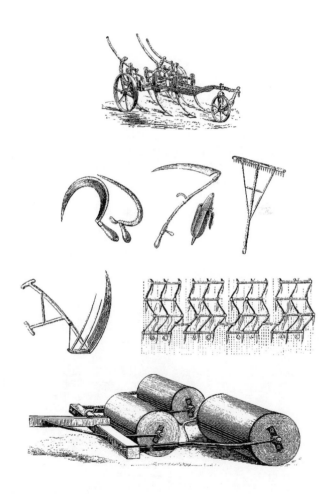

Could it take anything less than a cast of thousands—or *millions*—to picture the work of Christ? And perhaps we are still in the early days.

21

A cast of thousands

DEALING WITH THE DUST DEVIL

*And God said to him, "I am God Almighty: be fruitful and
multiply. A nation and a company of nations shall come
from you, and kings shall come from your own body."*
(Genesis 35:11)

THE BIBLE MATRIX DEMONSTRATES THE "fractal" nature of
history. Sure, history repeats itself. Everyone knows that.
But our personal histories are microcosms of the lives and
deaths of families, churches, nations and empires.

TORNADO OF DUST

The structure of events in the primeval Garden are
replayed in Cain and Abel, then in the sons of God.
Garden; Land; World. Most Holy; Holy; Courts. Word;
Sacrament; Government.

The pattern of creation was repeated in Adam and Eve,
Word becoming flesh, but instead of the building of a

greater Tabernacle out of raw materials, the dust devil of sin grew into a tornado, multiplying in speed and size, collecting material and taking on a body of its own—the entire race but for Noah and his family.

Jesus reversed the pattern in the Garden, but it took all of the Old Testament age to teach us—using types—what He would actually accomplish for this age. We need to analyze all the occurrences of the pattern, all the different ways in which it was played out in history, to comprehend every glorious facet of His redemptive achievement.

Just as death entered the entire world by the act of one man, it literally took a cast of thousands to portray the work of the Second Man. Cain slew Abel at the cross. Eve bore Seth as a replacement son in the resurrection. Enoch walked with God and "was not" at the ascension. Jonathan abdicated the Old Covenant and was resurrected as a New Covenant robe in David. Jephthah and David conquered as *"Conquest"* Land kings but had to die and be resurrected as *"Glorification"* World kings in Samson and Solomon respectively.

God took hold of Solomon's kingdom, divided it and then scattered it in judgment, but scattered its people as holy seed. This enlarged His field.

Jesus came to harvest this greater field. But the body of sin was also now much larger. By the time of Jesus, the sin that was dealt with in the exile had again taken on a body, become institutionalized, "corporate."

The compromise between the Jewish sons of God and the Gentile daughters of men was empire-wide. Just as Lamech's sin became institutionalized and ended the race, Ahab and Jezebel were incarnate in the draconian church-state of the Herods. This religio-political construct was an awesome body, but still an Adamic body of dust whose life was in the wind.

TORNADO OF BLOOD

Jesus dealt with the cyclone by standing in the eye. His ministry itself took on a body, but in the gospels we see Him whittle it away until He stands alone and rejected. The crowds abandon Him, and then even His band of brothers is scattered. His seamless robe, a symbol of His kingdom, is taken away. It also symbolized the Covenant—the firmament. The firmament is a garment for God, filled with governing lights. No lights (disciples), no robe. Jesus is torn from the Father, and then, more alone than anyone until the final judgment, Jesus' body itself is torn. All glory, all identity was gone, right down to the most personal, the most precious, the Most Holy.

He had no form or majesty that we should look at him, and no beauty that we should desire him. (Isaiah 53:2)

"The guards came again, handing out coats. I could not understand at first why they took away all of our clothes only to give us in return garments that must have been worn by other women entering the [concentration] camp. But as I looked around at the women beside me withdrawn into their meager, worn rags, I saw that we were no longer the strong women who had been able to endure hard labor, wartime conditions, and separation from our family and friends. The shearing of our heads and vulvas, the stealing of our clothes and everything we had owned, took from us the last traces of who we had been. My knapsack on the train, my mother's chains and rings, would never be given back. I felt their loss almost as much as the loss of my hair. All I had left was Samuel's ring.

When the guard reached me she held out a long gray coat. Without thinking I took it from her with my right hand. Immediately the guard circled the ring with her fingers and thumb, giving it a hard yank. My finger felt as if it were being pulled from me. The ring would not come off. Her grip tightened; the flesh around the ring was squeezed tightly. I cried out in pain.

'Quiet!' she hissed.

Again she pulled, spitting on the ring twice while she wiggled it back and forth. Finally, in one smooth movement, she scraped it over the ridge of my knuckle and slipped it off the end of my finger and into her pocket. Satisfied that no one had seen her, she shoved her crate of coats forward and moved on."[1]

Crowds torn away. Family torn away. Disciples torn apart. Robe torn off. Beard torn off. Body torn … veil torn … torn … torn *open*. And, in the most exquisite plot twist in history, the plunderer was plundered. In the eye of the cyclone, in the Most Holy Place, the Gordian knot was cut.

In the eye of the cyclone, in the tomb, Jonathan became David. A new history, begun with this one-Man liturgy, was spoken into the Garden. Over the next forty years, the kingdom of the father of lies began to unravel in the Land. As in the climax of "Peter and the Wolf," the more the Cunning Edomite Fox struggled, the tighter became the Apostolic rope around its neck.

Over the next forty years, Jesus took on a new body by His Spirit, and David became Solomon. Both John's Old Covenant decrease and Jesus' New Covenant increase became institutional. The headless Jonathan/John had a new Head.[2]

> *When his soul makes an offering for guilt, he shall see his offspring; he shall prolong his days.* (Isaiah 53:10)

The Word that tore open the Garden door began to tear open the Land. Revelation 14 shows Jesus again at the eye

1   Sarah Tuvel Bernstein, *The Seamstress, A Memoir of Survival*, pp. 198-199.
2   King Saul, Jonathan's "head," was beheaded.

of a cyclone. This time He is an Angel with a sickle. The literary structure puts Him at the beginning, middle and end. James Jordan writes:

> Six angels appear in this chapter. Four are from the 24 arch-angels, while two are the Angel of the Lord, the "Other Angel":

1. Jesus as Angel,		14:6
2. Archangel,		14:8
3. Archangel,		14:9
4. **Jesus as Man**,		14:14
5. Archangel,		14:15
6. Archangel,		14:17
7. Jesus as Angel,		14:18[3]

Sitting enthroned, right at the centre, Jesus is told that the time had come for His new "Land" body to follow Him through death and resurrection. The sickle swings and He harvests the saints as bread and wine. Now it was not just the eye but the whole Roman/Herodian cyclone that was red. What He accomplished on the cross was reenacted—filled up—in a cast of thousands. The empire was filled with violence and the corrupted sons of God disappeared beneath a flood of troops.[4]

---

3   James B. Jordan, *The Vindication of Jesus Christ*, p. 62.
4   See Peter J. Leithart, *Jewish War*, www.leithart.com

The band of brothers we join is one of blood brothers. More Christians were martyred in the twentieth century than in the previous nineteen centuries combined. As the victory in the Land continues to tear the World in two, the cast of thousands is now a cast of millions. Thankfully, the blood is always foundational. Spirit follows. But we must be ready with our blood.

Could it take anything less than a cast of thousands— or *millions*—to picture the work of Christ? And perhaps we are still in the early days.

> *Out of the anguish of his soul he shall see and be satisfied;*
> *by his knowledge shall the righteous one, my servant,*
> *make many to be accounted righteous, and he shall bear*
> *their iniquities. (Isaiah 53:11)*

What's on the table
is not what's
glorious. It's just a
memorial, a token,
the foundation
plaque on the
living house.

22

The glory are we

Then all the people shouted with a great shout, when they praised the Lord, because the foundation of the house of the Lord was laid. But many of the priests and Levites and heads of the fathers' houses, old men who had seen the first temple, wept with a loud voice when the foundation of this temple was laid before their eyes. (Ezra 3:11-12 NKJV)

Douglas Wilson writes:

> The Bible teaches us that the times of the new covenant are attended with a greater glory than the old covenant, as well as with a greater simplicity. In effect, that simplicity is part of the glory.
>
> The arrival of Jesus the Messiah was not a signal for us to lapse into some kind of second-rate old covenant observance. The old covenant was glorious, in its time, but when we try to imitate the types and shadows, we are dragging the lesser glory into something inglorious.
>
> This applies to many things—the sacrificial system, the practice of tithing, our observance of the Lord's Day, and so on. In place of the entire Mosaic economy, we have two sacraments. In place of a year of calendar obligations, we have one day of obligation, recurring

every seven days, and that recurrence is for the sake of our relief and rest. In place of bloody sacrifices, we have a cup of wine. In place of meat on the altar, we have a simple piece of bread.

The glory of the new covenant is simpler, but this simplicity is not to be understood as a downgrade. This simplicity is a relief, and an ornament of grace. It is not that we are barred from the glory that our old covenant brothers enjoyed, but rather that we are taught the meaning of a deeper glory. It is not as though God thinks that extra embroidery on Aaron's robe would be more glorious, but He doesn't want us to have that. Rather, God is teaching us that in the realm of glory, as with other forms of aesthetic experience, less is more.[1]

This is true enough but there is an important element missing from the observation. As we follow the patterns through the Bible, we find Word becoming Flesh. Every glorious element of the Tabernacle was a symbol to be fulfilled in, and constructed out of, people. The Restoration era is both difficult and interesting because it was a halfway house of sorts between the Old and New Covenants.

When the second Temple was built, the young people shouted and the old people wept. The young people got it right. Solomon's Temple was made of stone and wood.

---

1   Douglas Wilson, *Less Glory Is More*, www.dougwils.com

Ezekiel's Temple was made out of people. All New Jerusalems are.

The sacraments are not condensed or "deconstituted" versions of the Old Covenant glories. These ritual glories have taken on flesh by the Spirit of God. What is on the table is not what is glorious. It is just a memorial, a token, the foundation plaque on the living house.

Building the house took blood, sweat and tears. Since the end of the Old Covenant, Jesus is now going about His business filling the house. Israel sitting in the gates was only a preliminary glory. The nations entering the gates of Zion is a different kind of glory.

The Old and New Covenants, like everything else God seems to do, are a head and body. Adam builds the house and Eve fills it. Man is structure, woman is glory. Faithful Adams picture the beauty of self-sacrifice, but it is fitting that grace and forgiveness are the surpassing beauty of faithful Eve.

An Adam
governed
by God's Law
is an Adam
fit to govern.

23

Eye and tooth

*And God said, "Behold, I have given you every plant yield-ing seed that is on the face of all the earth, and every tree with seed in its fruit. You shall have them for food. And to every beast of the earth and to every bird of the heavens and to everything that creeps on the earth, everything that has the breath of life, I have given every green plant for food."
And it was so.* (Genesis 1:29-30)

"Every moving thing that lives shall be food for you. And as I gave you the green plants, I give you everything."
(Genesis 9:3)

SINCE THE CURSE FOR ADAM'S SIN WAS A DIVINE ACT of "de-Creation," we can't accurately imagine what the pre-Fall world was like. If there was no death for Adam, was there animal death? And if there was animal death, was there death for things like bacteria? Thankfully, the rest of the Bible does give us some clues.

It seems to me that the domestic and wild animals, those described as "breathing" and "living," wouldn't have died. Animals did not eat each other, and humans did not

169

eat animals. They were members of a single household, an image of heaven on earth.

Like God's throne, Adam's throne was surrounded by beasts. If he was faithful, as God is, they would submit and come to him for shelter, as God's beasts do, and as Noah's beasts did. They would become ministers of his wisdom.

Sin divides, sin cuts. Death was evidence of the judgment of sin. Eyes judge things to be good or evil, and horns and teeth carry out the judgment. This goes for animals and for people. Without a righteous Adam, glorious eyes, horns and teeth become instruments of death.

As with the Law concerning Adam and the Kingly Tree, and Israel's restricted diet, perhaps the animals also were temporarily prohibited by God from carrying out such judgments. The Law itself is "eye for eye, and tooth for tooth." Consequently, when Adam stole the kingly food, the hierarchy of the animal kingdom was bound with a chain—a *food* chain.

Those original animals, and humans, were consumers, and were not consumed. Everything else was consumable, until death entered by sin. Then *everything* became prey, subject to eye and tooth, especially after the Flood.

An Adam governed by God's Law is an Adam fit to govern. Noah put himself under God's Law. After his qualification through the Flood, he became the first Adam who was authorized to judge wisely and carry out

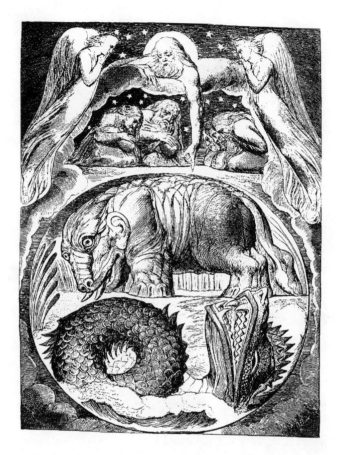

an execution. Now it was not only the Lord who consumed animals. Men did too, with eye and tooth, as judges under and over—that is, *mediating*—God's Law.

Jesus died under the Law, now He rules the world. After His qualification, He became a lamb with seven eyes and seven horns. Like Noah, the Father has put all things in subjection to Him; given Him "all things" to consume.

What was Moses reflecting? The great white throne of Greater Solomon, of course, the brilliant legal glory of Yahweh. Solomon's throne was covered in ivory.

24

Horns of Moses

GIVE US MEAT TO EAT

And whanne Moises cam doun fro the hil of Synai, he
helde twei tablis of witnessyng, and he wiste not that his
face was horned of the felouschipe of Goddis word.
(Exodus 34:29, Wycliffe)

PERHAPS YOU'VE SEEN THE BUMPER STICKER which says, *"If*
we're not meant to eat animals, why are they made of meat?"

It seems men didn't eat flesh until after the Flood. The
history from Adam to Noah follows the Feasts pattern,
with Adam as the "Alpha male" and Noah as the mature
and wise Omega male of that initial process.

Moving from vegetarianism (literally "seeds") to meat
was not only a sign of judgment, but a sign of *greater*
authority put into the hands of God's Man. Noah could eat
meat, and he could also sentence murderers to death.

Meat eating is kingly. It pictures judicial maturity
(Hebrews 5:12). Even under the New Covenant, a

temporary abstinence from "strong food" is for priestly purposes.

> It is good not to eat meat or drink wine or do anything that causes your brother to stumble. (Romans 14:21)

As members of a royal priesthood, we do not covet the place of honor at feasts (Matthew 23:6), or serve ourselves greedily at love feasts (Jude 1:12). Instead, we forego our "kingdom rights" for the exaltation of the Body.

> I ate no delicacies, no meat or wine entered my mouth, nor did I anoint myself at all, for the full three weeks. (Daniel 10:3)

Thanks to Noah's maturity, Man now had teeth in a way he had never had them before. Even we moderns use the word "toothless" to describe ineffective pieces of legislation. Teeth and tusks and ivory and horns are symbols of justice, whether they be on men, animals, or altars. If, on the very first Day of Coverings, Adam and Eve were clothed in the skins of a bull and a goat respectively, it would have been fitting for the Lord to display the four bloodied horns on the ground as a legal witness.[1] A blood-covered horn means the crime is atoned for.

Just as Christ was a Lamb with seven horns, worthy to open the scroll, Moses came down from Sinai with not only a "scroll" (or tablets in that case) but "horns." This translation has been dismissed as errant, but perhaps the reason for it should not be dismissed so easily. Here's my attempt at an interpretation.

Moses' face *shone*. He didn't actually have horns despite the many depictions of him with such in various paintings and sculptures. But the primary meaning of the Hebrew word from which this word "shone" is derived really is "horned." What was Moses reflecting? The great white throne of Greater Solomon, of course, the brilliant legal glory of Yahweh. Solomon's throne was covered in ivory.

An unrighteous Adam who faces God is gored by the horns of justice. If we don't judge rightly we will be judged. The blood of animals was substituted and displayed as a covering so that the High Priestly "Adam" could approach. As a righteous Adam (or a man covered by the blood), Moses received this legal glory. He became the Law-Word incarnate, the moon reflecting the sun in the night time of the Old Covenant, a glimpse of the glory to come in Christ.

Christ, of course, combined these two Adamic images. He was a lamb slain, but also a living lamb with seven

---

1   This might explain the three tusks/horns in the mouth of the Persian bear in Daniel 7:5. Jordan suggests that are they Daniel, Nehemiah and Mordecai—remnants of the throne of Solomon enabling Persia to devour the world. In the Bible, it's the good angels (cherubim) that have the horns, and Daniel's four beasts surrounded the throne of a resurrected Jew-Gentile kingdom, the *oikoumene*. This, of course, predicted "the age to come", the Gospel age, in which Satan not only has no horns, but as the accuser he is now toothless. It is now we who have the teeth and the horns—the Gospel.

horns. He was the ultimate satisfaction of God's brilliant justice, then He became the minister of that justice against the unrepentant ministers of the Old Creation order. He would even call Tyre, Sidon, Sodom and Gomorrah as witnesses against the Jewish leaders when the time came.

So the word "horned" is possibly a deliberate play on words, or the use of a word that combined two meanings: *shining* and *law*. Moses was a horned altar, Sinai as a man, with a face as white and hard as enamel—a face like a flint. Under his judgment, the righteous would be vindicated and the wicked destroyed. The threshing (chewing) process would leave only two men alive, a number which didn't even include Moses: Joshua and Caleb, two spies, two witnesses—two eyes.

Under this new Levitical Law, a new "Garden" would be constructed, and a great many animals would be slaughtered and offered within its insatiable boundary. It was a King's Table. Yahweh was *already* Omega, *already* Solomon. But the people of Israel, not yet humbled enough to possess the Land, desired Omega food, the food of "ascension," for themselves.[2] Not satisfied with the sweet bread of "priestly" obedience, they lobbied for meat to eat and were themselves consumed.

---

2   In Exodus 24, Moses and the elders feasted with the Lord as kings (Exodus 24:9-11). It was the end of the "Egypt" cycle. However, when Moses ascended Sinai to receive the Law, he fasted (Exodus 24:18). He was "eaten" as a priest. It was the beginning of a new cycle.

Horned man

"Something to check: Is Moses the first 'horned man' in the Bible? He comes down from the mountain, having seen the glory of God, with 'horns' on his head, rays of glory radiating out. This may be the source of the horned man image used elsewhere, in the Psalms for instance: He has raised up my horn like a wild ox and God has raised up a horn of salvation for us in the house of his servant David. It may also be the source of the 'horned crown' image; many crowns in antiquity and the middle ages were stylized horns, suggesting a radiation of glory from the head of the king."

— Peter J. Leithart, www.leithart.com

Touching a bone made an Israelite unclean. Burning bones upon Jeroboam's altars defiled them. This was not because bones were unholy but because they were already holy.

25

Bone and flesh

STRUCTURE AND GLORY

This is now bone of my bones and flesh of my flesh;
She shall be called Woman, because she was taken out of Man.
(Genesis 2:23)

ALL OF HISTORY IS A PROCESS OF PARTING AND REUNION.
What was accomplished in Genesis 1 "creationally" is
reflected in Genesis 2 "socially." W. H. Auden observes
that in Genesis 1, Man is described as a natural creature,
"subject like all other creatures to the laws of the natural
order." In Genesis 2, however, Man is defined "as a unique
individual who desires and is capable of entering into
unique relations with others."[1]

ADAM'S BOSOM

The structure of Genesis 2, like Genesis 1, follows the
order of Israel's feasts. It puts the cutting of Adam and the

---

1   Arthur Kirsch, *Auden and Christianity,* pp. 116-117.

construction of Eve at *Atonement*. Adam was the High Priest whose "garment of glory" was temporarily removed to clothe the Bride. His "linen skin" was bloodied to buy a future for his people.

The Land was "decreased" that the glory of the world might be "increased." Likewise, Adam was "decreased" that Eve, his glory, might be "increased." A rib was removed, but from where was it removed, and why?

The bone was taken from his chest, his bosom, because this is the place where the Great Servant carries the people of God. Here Greater Eve finds rest "socially" until Greater Adam carries her into the freedom of God's rest "creationally." Lazarus rested in Abraham. John rested in Jesus.

GOD'S WHITENER

Men are *structure*. Women are *glory*. Bones are *structure*. Flesh and fat are *glory*. Law is structure. Grace is glory. Law is bones. Grace is flesh. And fat.

Touching a bone made an Israelite unclean. Burning bones upon Jeroboam's altars defiled them—not because bones were unholy but because they were already *holy*.

In the field, bones could not be touched. They were not to be burned as an offering to God. If they were burned, they were burned on pagan altars as a confirmation of judgment (a second legal witness), or burned to lime and used to mark memorials and graves. Bones were refused by God, neither are they eaten by men. Unlike flesh, they neither bring life to us nor reproduce. Like the limed stones on Mount Ebal, they can only testify to a life that has passed away under the curse of the Law (Deuteronomy 27:2-4). When the bones of Saul and his house were buried, God lifted the curse from the Land (2 Samuel 21). Interestingly, the law concerning the touching of bones alludes to the construction of Eve.

> Whoever *(Initiation - Ark)*
> > touches *(Delegation - Veil)*
> > > in the open field *(Elevation - Altar)*
> > > > one who is slain by a sword *(Presentation - Table)*
> > > > > or who has died, *(Purification - Lampstand)*
> > > > or a bone of a man, *(Transformation - Incense)*
> > > or a grave, *(Vindication - Mediators)*
> > shall be unclean seven days. *(Representation - Shekinah)*
> (Numbers 19:16)

Notice the progression from sword/flesh (Sacrifice), to death (Curse of the Law), to a bone of "Adam" (White Witness), to grave (Day of Coverings). Not only does this stipulation follow the same structure as Genesis 2, it also follows the sacrificial process, the Feasts, and the Tabernacle furniture. The High Priest himself was a Tabernacle, and the Incense Altar corresponds to the 12 gemstones on his 24 "bridal" ribs. Bones are holy as long as they are clean of Adamic flesh.

STONES AND BONES

The bones of sinners could be broken. Stones from the Land would rise up and "cover them," gnashing upon them like teeth. The bodies of sinners would be completely torn down, not one stone left upon another.

However, an intact skeleton was a "house of death," an old Tabernacle made white inside and out, cleaned by scavengers. The bones of the Passover Lamb were not to be broken. Like the bones of Christ (John 19:36), they were a testimony to the end of the Old Covenant body and the promise of a new one.

Likewise, the old leaven, the old "flesh," was completely cut off. Bones are the past. Flesh is the future. And flesh can be holy or unholy.

When an Israelite's skin plague had covered his body, he was no longer unclean but holy (Leviticus 13:12-14). The curse was complete. Flesh offered to God must be blameless, white, a Covenant Body presented as a "chaste virgin" to the Father.

HOLY SMOKE

As with the leper, raw flesh symbolized an incomplete work of the Law. Flesh that is unholy can be made clean, given new life, through transformation by holy fire.

Adulterers and murderers were to be stoned to death. But the adulterous daughter of a priest was to be stoned and *then* burned with fire. She could be purified, made chaste in her death, just like Jerusalem. Eve, like flesh, is always the future. She is the mother of multiplication, a complex body of fragrant smoke.

Two Kinds of White

Teeth and horns are the whiteness of the Law. The Law can only execute judgment. The Law cannot bring new life. The whiteness of the Law is the whiteness of the sepulcher, the whiteness of the grave marker, the whiteness of the stone from the Ephod which declared that the covering, the atonement offering, had been accepted for another year. It is also the whiteness of Lot's wife, the purity of sterility and disinfection. The whiteness of bones testifies that the Law has been *satisfied*. It is the whiteness of death. The ground no longer cries out. The curse is complete. Adam has returned to the dust.

But there is also a whiteness of life. The white hair and white robes of the elder are a sign that the Law has been *obeyed and internalized*. He is a rib whose individual holiness will found a new body. Saints, as elders, continually put on the white robes of Christ, our older brother, as a body for the wisdom and righteousness of God.

The Valley of Bones

The knife of God cut into Adam until He discovered internal whiteness. Likewise, all the "Old Covenants" cut away at the flesh of corporate Adam, whittling mankind down to one nation, one tribe, one family, one naked individual, until God found the whiteness He desired.

God did the same with Joseph. Jacob's sons were "cut away" until a blameless son was found. Joseph went willingly into the grave of Egypt and emerged with a new body. His bones were holy, and God brought them out of the grave with new flesh, a new body for Israel.

But Israel sinned. In Jeremiah 8, God promised to scatter the bones of her leaders before the sun, moon and stars they had worshiped. They would be a testimony that the Law of Moses was satisfied. Ezekiel predicts the new bride, an army called from the dust, bones covered in flesh, then filled with the Spirit. The rebirth of Israel would be just as it was in Eden. She was again called "out of man," prepared as a bride adorned for her husband.

We are tombs full of dead men's bones, but they are now the incorruptible bones of Joseph, of Jesus. The Spirit carries them out of the grave in a new body, a holy army. In the secret place, flesh and bone and blood are miraculously knitted together.

However, ours is a better Adam. We are not only bone of His bones, and flesh of His flesh, but also Spirit of His Spirit.

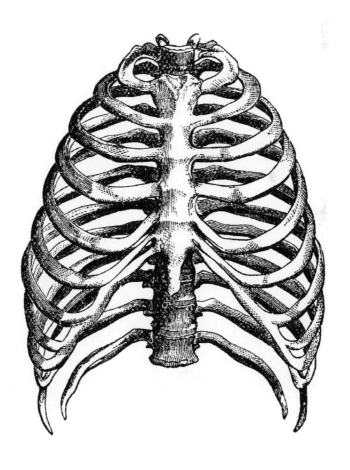

As in Eden, atonement
was an unfair barter,
an unequal exchange,
in which God was
happy to be ripped off.

26

Skin for skin

THE REVELATION OF ADAM

Then Satan answered the Lord and said, "Skin for skin! All that a man has he will give for his life." (Job 2:4)

ONE ASPECT OF ALLOWING THE BIBLE to interpret the world for us is to see the significance of things. Modern evangelicals generally pass off the weird references to things like bone, flesh and skin as though they were part of an outmoded worldview. But, despite all appearances, modern scholars are themselves yet made of bone, flesh and skin. These things are significant in the created order. They communicate something to us. Bone is structure, flesh is life, and skin is glory. It is a three-level Tabernacle: Garden, Land, World, or Word, Sacrament, Government.

Just as heaven has three levels, and its reflected glory in the earth has three levels, so too does the Mediator. A human is mind (Word), body (Sacrament) and movement (arms and legs: Government). But the Body itself, as

Mediator, has three levels, bone, flesh and skin. The Body is the Tabernacle mediating between heaven and earth. The Israelites were a nation of mediators, of living Sacraments. Concerning priestly duties, even the purity of their skin mattered (Leviticus 13).

But there is the third level, Government, so we still require clothing. In the Bible, robes are the "official skin," a sign of one's visible office or role in the social world. A robed man is a judge, a husband and a father. He is a servant with the authority of his master.

The Lord used skin to make tunics for Adam and Eve. The Hebrew word is singular, so James Jordan says it was a single animal, a single mediator picturing Christ. He is probably right, but based on later events, it is possible that a bull was killed for Adam and a goat or two for Eve, prefiguring the Day of Coverings (Atonement). It would then have been the Lord, not the animal, as the Single Mediator, the High Priest making two approaches: one to cover the head (Adam), and another to cover the body (Eve). This means there would have been blood shed twice. Can this be linked to the death of Christ? Yes, it can, and in a way that few Bible expositors see because they won't recognize repeated patterns.

The complete structure of the ministry of Christ includes the murder of the Firstfruits (Apostolic) Church. Jordan thinks this is the abomination of desolation, more literally, the "desecrating sacrilege," and the repeated structures of the Bible bear this out.

This was the blood of the body, the first goat. It allowed all of God's wrath to be poured out upon the second goat, the Jewish rulers, their precious Temple and their corrupted church-state. This ended the animal sacrifices. It ended the history of temporary covering begun in Genesis 3.

THE HOUSE OF DEATH

The proto-Temple, the Tabernacle, was covered in skins. Inside it was glorious. Outside it was not. The skins of the sacrificial animals were never worn by Israelites. These were always given to the priests. These skins were evidence of a justice that was satisfied. Adam presents himself to the Father, and then presents his "covered" bride.

> Then the man said, "This at last is bone of my bones and flesh of my flesh; she shall be called Woman, because she was taken out of Man." Therefore a man shall leave his father and his mother and hold fast to his wife, and they shall become one flesh. And the man and his wife were both naked and were not ashamed. (Genesis 2:23-25)

Her purity is evidence of his Covenant faithfulness. But Adam hid himself, and his bride, under a false covering.

So, the dead animal/s were evidence of Covenant faithfulness. *Or were they?* No, they were a trick. The Day of

Coverings is a trick. Joseph's brothers covered his robe in goat's blood and presented it to Jacob as false evidence. Jacob himself had worn the skins of goats to fool Isaac. The flesh of the goats was also used as part of Rebekah's deception. Michal used a goat skin to stall David's pursuers long enough for him to escape. All of these pictures show an apparent miscarriage of justice by God. The judgment falls, for sure. But the curse falls upon the substitute.

As Peter Leithart has observed, the Tabernacle and Temple were like *The Picture of Dorian Gray*. The house of God, the house of skins, absorbed the judgment of God, keeping it at bay by sacrificing innocent animals. As in Eden, the curse of death did fall.

When Israel herself became a murderess, under the Kings of Israel and Judah and later under the Edomite Herods, it was also a Covenant trick. The shepherds were wolves hiding in the skins of sheep. This is Cainite worship, and it goes right back to the system of vengeance set up by Lamech. The house of mercy for all nations becomes a house of vengeance, a house that does not absorb death but *meted it out.*

> For with the judgment you pronounce you will be judged, and with the measure you use it will be measured to you. (Matthew 7:2)

The blood that flowed from such a house was human. No human is innocent, but this blood was not a just recompense for crimes committed. It also forced God's hand to step in and judge the unmerciful, hard-hearted, corrupted sons of God for perverting His house. Paul warned the Jews in Rome against the hypocrisy of skin-deep religion:

> Or do you despise the riches of His goodness, forbearance, and longsuffering, not knowing that the goodness of God leads you to repentance? But in accordance with your hardness and your impenitent heart you are treasuring up for yourself wrath in the day of wrath and revelation of the righteous judgment of God. (Romans 2:4-5 NKJV)

Of course, God's house moved on in history from a tent covered in skins. It became a glorious house of stone, and eventually, under the Herods, a house covered in white stone and gold. However, "The Temple of the Lord" ceased to be a protection when the goodness of God did not lead to repentance. Did they realize their own Messiah was the painting hidden in the attic, the Innocent One upon whom the guilt of millennia of murders was being "treasured up," the One who could still say, "Father, forgive them; they don't know what they are doing"?

Here was the perfect trick, the ultimate deception. A supposed miscarriage of justice was an "eye for eye" deception of the serpent. Jesus shed the skin of sin, the pure linen garment spotted by the flesh. But He (or the angels) laid it out in two parts, like the ascension sacrifice: a head, and a body. Jesus was the Adam, the Covenant Head. The Firstfruits Church, the Covenant Body, would follow a generation later, "in like manner."

After the Jewish rulers murdered the Son, they set about murdering His Bride. Their final abomination was the slaying of Jewish Christians inside the city. The Roman armies put an end to the shedding of blood. The game of "animal hide" was over.

The final sacrifice had been made, so the House of Death was obsolete. It had been replaced by a new Temple, a House of Life. A Jewish heritage was now redundant. The only Jewish bloodline that ever mattered to God was now in heaven—Head *and* Body.

Upon those who rejected this final sacrifice, all the blood from Abel to Zechariah was avenged. At the same moment, Jesus presented the true Bride, His bloodied Joseph-robe, to the Father as evidence of His Covenant faithfulness.

THE HOUSE OF LIFE

They were stoned, they were sawn in two, they were killed with the sword. They went about in skins of sheep and goats, destitute, afflicted, mistreated... (Hebrews 11:37)

Israelites didn't normally wear animal skins. They were commanded to wear glorious robes with blue "wings" (tassels). Clothing was made of linen or wool, "fruits" of the Land (hair in the Bible is Bridal glory, not death). The circumcision of each Israelite pictured the House of Death. The robe of each Israelite himself personally pictured the future glory of the House of Resurrection. When the sacrificial system became corrupt, the Lord sent prophets—Adams—dressed in animal skins. They lived "cut off" in the wilderness. God was taking things back to scratch. He was tearing off the Bridal glory and exposing nakedness. Back to the skin, in fact, back to the foreskin—the bloodied Lamb at the foundation of the Bridal City. God would create a New Jerusalem, and He would make all things new with blood.

So, through the skin-covered prophets God demoted the kings of Israel back to serving as a priesthood within Gentile empires. The testimony of the prophets was a revealing, an "apocalypse." It was a new circumcision, a pruning that would cut off the old order and bring a new, more abundant life.[1]

---

1   This idea comes from Steven Opp's discussion of Paul's use of language in Galatians to describe the Gospel as a kind of "circumcision of the Circumcision" in his paper: *It's the End of the Flesh as we Know It! A Comparison of Circumcision & Apocalypse,* 2010. For the symbolic meanings of circumcision, see James B. Jordan, *The Law of the Covenant,* pp. 78-84.

All the various incarnations of Israel, except One, wanted resurrection without death, but this is impossible. God covered them with boils, head to foot, so they could again produce the fruits of faith. Skin for skin; stripes for salve. But it was only a token. As in Eden, atonement was an unfair barter, an unequal exchange, in which God was happy to be ripped off, to be skinned.

The Western Church is getting the boils. We are being stripped. We wanted end time Bridal glory without Garden obedience; kingdom without the temporary nakedness of the cross. We desire new wine from old skins, but we need new repentance and new mercy. We need prophets from the wild, Reformers who boldly wear the goodness and severity of God—men in fresh skins.

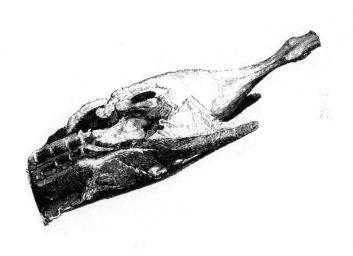

The blessing for obedience to the Covenant was dominion over the beasts... The Covenant curse, however, was to be *eaten* by them.

27

Birds and beasts

The Philistine said to David, "Come to me, and I will give your flesh to the birds of the air and to the beasts of the field." (1 Samuel 17:44)

Then Rizpah the daughter of Aiah took sackcloth and spread it for herself on the rock, from the beginning of harvest until rain fell upon them from the heavens. And she did not allow the birds of the air to come upon them by day, or the beasts of the field by night. (2 Samuel 21:10)

AT THE HEART OF THE BIBLE MATRIX IS *TESTING*. All the major narratives follow the pattern, and many of the minor ones do, too.

If Adam had not failed his initial "qualifying round," he would have progressed to the next stage of dominion. We know this because we see others later in the Bible move beyond this first round to greater glory. For instance, Daniel's first challenge mirrors Adam's challenge exactly. He was offered kingdom food and refused it.

Initially, the beasts which Adam was to subdue were *actual* beasts. As the history progresses, the pattern includes not only the beasts of the field but also the birds of the air and the beasts of the sea.

The blessing for obedience to the Covenant was dominion over the beasts. The animals willingly submit, which is exactly what we see in Noah, and typologically in Solomon, Jonah, Mordecai and Paul. The Covenant curse, however, was to be *eaten* by them. In the latter case, one's body was left unburied and exposed, allowed to "see" corruption.

WHERE DOMINION BEGINS

Before the beasts submit to Man, Man must submit to God. Notice that God's purifying judgment upon King Nebuchadnezzar was to make him a kind of Covenant-curse hybrid: both a beast and a bird. Only heavenly creatures are described as such "holy combinations." The Gentile king was being transformed into a guardian for God's people—a cherub. Only once he learned submission to God could he truly be "the Man."

Although the king's outward transfiguration was instant, his inward transformation took time. So often we plead for mastery in a particular domain and expect the Lord to change us miraculously in a single act. We could not be more mistaken.

The daily grind is designed to *enlarge us* to possess, to expand us to the point where our occupation of that

Birds and beasts

greater domain will be the most natural thing imaginable. All the saints, like David, have the hearts of potential kings. God requires us to be faithful in little before we can be faithful in much, and this usually means time in the wilderness, time under the dominion of birds and beasts.

A SLOW VICTORY

If God dealt with all our sins, called us to rule over every single fault, at conversion, we would most certainly die of fright. As food, He begins at the exterior and works His way in. As we eat the bread and drink the wine, we are both shown mercy and judged. Or rather, called to judge ourselves wisely.

That means greater testing, greater suffering, more humbling, more curly issues that require sound wisdom—and of course, more glory as we minister out of all this to others. The process is gradual.

> I will not drive them out from before you in one year, lest the land become desolate and the wild beasts multiply against you. Little by little I will drive them out from before you, until you have increased and possess the land. (Exodus 23:29-30)

WHERE DOMINION ENDS

This gradual process also applies to churches, nations and empires.

Jesus drove the demons out of Judah. He carried it out gradually over three years. What happened? Many Jews believed, culminating in Pentecost. But those Jews who refused to believe, who blasphemed the Holy Spirit even after the Pentecostal house was filled, were a house left clean, decorated and empty.[1] The beasts of the field, or in this case, seven worse demons, multiplied against Him, and its state was worse than the first. The demonic problem in the hearts of men grew to become a united, national scourge.

Rather than conquering the Greek and Roman empire "beasts" through faithful witness, the Herods worked to keep the Roman "Sea beast" in submission through a "beastly" compromise of the Covenant. The Revelation shows the Land Beast (the Herodian rulers) manipulating the power of the Sea Beast (Rome) to deceive the Covenant people. Eventually, their "cherubic" guardian devoured them.

As the Herodian priesthood refused its call to faithful guard duty, the Garden of Judaism, the Temple, was

---

1 In the Creation week, God formed the house over three days, then filled it over the next three. The filling begins at Day 4, feast 4, Pentecost, *Testing*.

finally overrun with the beasts of the field and the birds of the air. But all the while the number of saints across the empire was growing. The Revelation uses the symbols of the victory of Israel over Jericho to describe their final victory. The apostles were faithful in their witness, and God gave this increase.

What is highly ironic is that the Revelation describes the martyrdom of the Firstfruits Church and its aftermath with an interesting symbol. Their bodies were left *exposed* in the streets by those who thought this sect was *accursed,* by those who maintained that *they* were the true people of the Covenant. But these faithful saints, under the true Covenant, rose and ascended in plain sight. Like their Lord, like the atoning human sacrifices in 2 Samuel 10, they did not see corruption.

Don't sweat the birds and the beasts, personally or corporately. Although we are called to be watchful witnesses, the unconquered character faults, contrary people and scavenging nations will be dealt with in God's good time. The scaffolding is still up in every area. Obviously, the Church is not yet ready to rule the world and to judge angels. And neither are you. But don't ever doubt that that promised day is coming.

Under the
New Covenant,
the Church Herself
becomes the greatest
"scavenger" of all time.

28

The greatest consumer

NOW WE ARE GODS

THE DIETARY LAWS GIVEN TO MOSES were an expansion of
the command given to Adam. It is the self-denial of
priestly obedience to God. Adam wasn't ready for the tree
of judicial responsibility (kingdom) but he seized it.

In the greater Bible picture, Israel's history (from
Moses) is this period of priestly obedience. But Jesus came
and reversed Adam's failure.

Consequently the dietary laws are revoked, and with
greater maturity, the Church of God, like Jesus, now has
the judicial wisdom of the Spirit, and the power to eat
unclean things (Gentiles), consume them and make them
clean. Only the power of resurrection can enter a room
with a corpse in it, touch lepers, feast on Gentile meats
and not be made unclean, but instead make the unclean
clean by consuming it. This is New Covenant power.

This power only comes after obedience (in this case, obedience to the gospel). Fasting, then feasting.

Under the Old Covenant, scavengers were unclean demonic "servants" of God. Under the new, the Church Herself becomes the greatest "scavenger" of all time, the body of Christ eating the dead and incorporating them into His life by resurrection. Only those who will not die, will not judge themselves, those who are neither fire nor water, hot nor cold, are vomited out as unclean. Lukewarmness is the old life refusing to die. No death (fasting), means no resurrection (feasting). Jesus is our food, and we are His: we in Him, and He in us. Greater Solomon reigns, and the world is His table. Unlike Adam, Christ didn't seize the kingdom, so the Father gave it to Him on a platter.

Just as the unclean birds carried out the Covenant curses for God, now the Church of God is the great clean bird situated between heaven and earth, brooding over the abyss, devouring the corpses of those dead in transgressions and rendering them alive as they pass through her Laver gates. The crystal sea still dispenses angelic government, but now it is the crystal city, and the Advocate has replaced the Accuser.

Greater Daniel fasted, and now eats anything Babylon presents to Him. Greater Esther proclaimed a fast, but now devours even the twisted monsters of the deep and makes Gog and Magog fit for God. No nation is too unclean for resurrection. And no nation is strong enough to resist, for she devours and transforms them from the inside.

Little by little, the world passes through the Tabernacle of Jesus, dismembered, washed, burnt and ascended, until all is a holy aroma pleasing to God.

So fast and pray, then go out and eat (with) the unclean, remembering two things: firstly, that righteousness is an acquired taste; and secondly, that Jesus always keeps the best till the end.

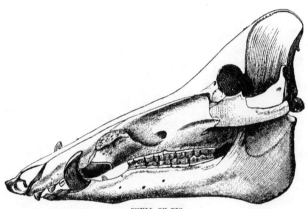

SKULL OF PIG.

Jesus desires
His new people
to be fire and
water, coming
out of Egypt.

29

Spat out at Jesus' table

I know your works: you are neither cold nor hot. Would that
you were either cold or hot! So, because you are lukewarm,
and neither hot nor cold, I will spit you out of my mouth.
(Revelation 3:15-16)

IN THE BOOK OF REVELATION, many sentences contain
multiple Old Testament allusions knotted together.
Sometimes these are more obvious, for example, the
Judaizers as Babylonian locusts from Joel with long hair
added to make them "bad Nazirites." However, sometimes
the allusions only become apparent from their position
within the literary structure of the passage in question.
The sequence of events is itself a clever allusion.

FEASTS

Laodicea is the seventh church. This puts it at the Feast of
Tabernacles (or Booths), to which the Gentiles were
invited. It also makes it the great feasting Table of

Solomon, the Sabbath king who had rest from all his enemies: the glorified Bridegroom. Here, Christ is greater Solomon, *but he's not happy with the food.*

HISTORY

The seven letters also recapitulate Israel's history. Sardis is the remnant during the great apostasy that ended up in Babylon. Philadelphia is the new Temple pillar in Ezra-Nehemiah's restoration. That makes Laodicea the period of compromise during which the Messiah was born. Laodicea represents the end of Adam's corrupted week— apostate Judaism. At Booths, a blameless Adam offers Himself as shelter before the old house is torn down.

GEOGRAPHY

Burial in the Land carried the promise of resurrection for the faithful. Unlike jaded Naomi, Ruth the Moabitess used the Lord's Covenant name (Yahweh), and wished to be buried in the Land as was Sarah.

The Church is a new Jerusalem and Jesus is the new Land. To be consumed by Him, baptized (immersed) into Him now carries this sure promise of resurrection. But for the unfaithful, just like the old Promised Land, it carries the threat of being vomited out, like the Jews in both the captivity and the first century.

Jesus' people were a new Israel, so He desired from

them the water and fire of sound judgment. He would consume them so He could "speak" them as living epistles. The completed Firstfruits Church was not vomited out of the Land. It *grew naturally* out of the Land.

THE LAW

The seven letters follow the Feasts structure, and each letter also follows this pattern internally. The letter to the Laodicean pastor exposes natural fire, water, and sight as impotent shadows and offers their spiritual realities:

A letter from "the beginning of God's Creation"
(Genesis - Sabbath)
    The Laodicean pastor is neither water nor fire
    (Exodus - Passover)
        Herod's carnal "Tabernacle" riches are corrupt
        (Leviticus - Firstfruits)
            Jesus offers gold refined by fire
            and white clothes (water)
            and clear sight (sound judgment)
            (Numbers - Pentecost)
        Those whom He loves He reproves
        (Deuteronomy - Trumpets)
    As High Priest, He knocks at the door
    (Joshua - Atonement)
He offers a throne to those who conquer
(Judges - Booths)

(A summary of Revelation 3:14-22)

211

The division between "hot and cold" comes at Passover/Exodus, alluding to the waters of the Red Sea and the pillar of fire. Jesus desired His new people to *be* fire and water, coming out of Egypt. Instead, they were being destroyed by fire and water.

> "Lord, have mercy on my son, *(Sabbath)*
>> for he is [moonstruck] *(Passover)*
>>> and he suffers terribly. *(Firstfruits)*
>>>> For often he falls into the fire, *(Pentecost)*
>>>> and often into the water.
>>> And I brought him to your disciples, *(Trumpets)*
>> and they could not heal him." *(Atonement)*
> *(No Booths)* (Matthew 17:15)

The Covenant structure means that the extreme temperatures Jesus expects in us are *ethical*. We consider His Laws, then He considers—*chews*—us to discover *internal* law: hatred of sin and love of righteousness.

If we overlay the pattern of sacrifice upon the letter, the lukewarm food appears at *Division,* the cutting of the sacrifice. Food is a sacrifice eaten by God. It must be blameless, holy. After being set apart, we are to draw near to God as holy sacrifices. James Jordan writes:

> Eating represents taking something into yourself and being united with it. In the Lord's supper we eat the flesh and drink the blood of Jesus Christ. In that way, we are united to Him. In Revelation 3, Jesus says "because

you are lukewarm I will spit you out of my mouth," which means that He is also eating us, and we are incorporated into the body of Christ.[1]

Added to this is the warning to Peter in Acts, which he heeded. "Rise Peter; kill and eat." Peter at first refused to eat unclean animals.

> Unclean animals represented unconverted Gentiles. Clean, non-sacrificial animals like gazelle, deer, chicken and fish represented Gentile God-fearers. The sacrificial animals—goat, sheep, pigeon, dove and bull— represented Israelites. This system represented the different nations of the world, and Peter sees them all inside this vessel. The Lord says, "What God has cleansed, you shall not defile." Peter is the source of uncleanness, and Peter has the potential to defile Cornelius... If Peter's attitude of hostility towards Gentiles continued, based on the artificial barriers the Jews had added to the Law, *he* would defile *them*. [2]

Compromisers and Judaizers were now the defiling animals. The letter ends with the faithful dining with Jesus in His new Tabernacle at the marriage feast of the Lamb.

---

1   James B. Jordan, *Select Studies in Acts* lectures. Available from
      www.wordmp3.com
2   Jordan.

Molech was simply another dragon hijacking the offspring of the woman with an offer of certain food.

30

Kids in the kitchen

PASSOVER IN THE MOTHERLAND

You shall not boil a young goat in its mother's milk.
(Exodus 23:19)

*And alas for women who are pregnant and for those who
are nursing infants in those days!* (Matthew 24:19)

FATHERHOOD AND MOTHERHOOD ARE DIFFERENT BLESSINGS.
The father initiates life and the mother brings it to pass.
The father is a husbandman, the farmer, and the mother
personifies the land. The word for "land" in Hebrew is
feminine. The father protects the land, nourishes it, and
tends it, so the land can bring forth an increase from God.
Subsequently, the corruption of fatherhood and motherhood bring different curses.

The Old Testament is the history of the battle between
the offspring of the woman and the offspring of the
serpent. It is a history of barrenness and fruitfulness. As a
new Eden, Israel frequently suffered barren Land and

215

barren wombs, and it took the love, mercy and power of God to make her fruitful again. In her final years, it was a virgin's womb that God made impossibly fruitful, and the words of her Offspring sent the entire Land into birth pangs.

There are two kinds of men in the Bible, shepherds and wolves. There are also two kinds of mother; a mother who lays down her life for her children, as her husband lays down his life for her, and there is the mother who has no natural affection, hardened by the abuse of evil men.

The command against boiling a kid in its mother's milk is an enigma designed to horrify us as we chew upon it. The very means of the infant's life becomes its shroud in death. However, it is not a dietary law. James Jordan writes:

> The law forbidding boiling a kid in its own mother's milk is not properly a food law at all. Obviously, if one is not to boil the kid, one is not to eat it either, but this is not what the law explicitly states. It is the very act of boiling, quite apart from the eating, that is forbidden. This can reasonably be extended to boiling the young of any animal in its own mother's milk, and that is as far as reasonable inference can take us. Had God intended to prohibit cooking meat and milk, He would have phrased the law that way on at least one of the three occasions He caused it to be recorded.[1]

1   James B. Jordan, *Studies in Food and Faith,* "On Boiling Meat in Milk."

Jordan observes that the command is associated with the Feast of Tabernacles, and "with a general theology of sabbath, success, and inheritance." The Feast of Tabernacles was a celebration of the fullness of life. Boiling a kid in its mother's milk was a mixing of life and death.[2]

Just as the Passover sacrifice of a lamb or kid redeemed a human child, so a kid boiled in its mother's milk for this final feast pictured the deliberate foiling of human succession. It was the sacrifice of a permanent blessing on the altar of a temporary gain. Lamentations 4:10 and 2 Kings 6:28-29 both record mothers boiling their own children and eating them.

> And the king asked her, "What is your trouble?" She answered, "This woman said to me, 'Give your son, that we may eat him today, and we will eat my son tomorrow.' So we boiled my son and ate him. And on the next day I said to her, 'Give your son, that we may eat him.' But she has hidden her son." (2 Kings 6:28-30)

The forbidden combination of kid and milk is a sick parody of motherhood, and it pictures the state of Israel at her most corrupt. Imitating the Canaanite practice, Israel attempted to secure abundant crops from Baal through the means of child sacrifice. This lawless mixture of

---

2 Psalm 8 is a 7 x 7 in its structure. It is interesting that "nursing infants" is placed at the Booths/Tabernacles step of its second cycle (Passover).

blessing and cursing, life and death, is a corporate outworking of the events recorded in Genesis 3. Molech was simply another dragon hijacking the offspring of the woman with an offer of certain food (kingdom) outside of priestly obedience to the Law of God.

Eve's seduction brought death to all her children. Adam stood by and watched, concerned with only his immediate advantage. As they consumed the fruit from the tree of the knowledge of good and evil, they consumed the promises of God: the fruit of the Land and the fruit of the womb. Their succession became an unnatural mixture of life and death. The Land promised to Adam now suffered slavery to sin.

Covenant history is not merely a search for the *Offspring* of the Woman. We are also given numerous examples of Covenant men given the tough job of discerning the identity of the *true Mother.*

Abraham chose wisely between Hagar and Sarah, the naturally fertile Egyptian bondwoman and the miraculously fertile Covenant freewoman. It was a distasteful choice, but one mother was the past and one mother was the future. One was Egypt and the other was Canaan.

Solomon became famous for the wisdom he employed in his discernment between the two prostitutes. The threat of cutting the living child in two revealed the hearts of both women. The true mother was a true mother—a mother not only in flesh but in spirit. This woman was a shelter, willing to suffer loss to be a human Tabernacle. To save her child, she volunteered to let her child go. The sword "cuts the cord." Hers was the faith of Abraham.

Judah suffered under the rule of Athaliah, who willingly slaughtered her grandchildren to usurp the throne of her dead son. This was a reverse succession, an unwillingness to allow Covenant history to move forward. She would sacrifice the fruit of the womb for a stolen throne.

The festival that the Jews consistently failed to appreciate was the Feast of Tabernacles. It was the feast that reminded them that they were not an elite people but a nation of priests called apart by God to serve the other nations. The New Testament records the unwillingness of the Jewish rulers to submit to the fulfillment of Tabernacles, a feast where Jew and Gentile were united under God. The fact that the feast which characterized the celebration of the completion of Herod's Temple was not Tabernacles but Passover highlights the nature of Herodian rule—theirs was a stolen throne.[3]

The infants of Israel should have been safe in their motherland. But Herod the Great slaughtered the offspring of Israel according to the flesh, and the final Herod slaughtered the Church, the offspring of Israel

---

3   For a discussion of the contrast between Passover and Tabernacles, see chapter 5, *Eat Local and Die.*

according to the Spirit. First century Israel was revealed by Jesus to be another Egypt (Revelation 11:8).

Herod's slaughter of the innocents gives us the key to the strange law concerning boiling a kid in its mother's milk. It is a confusion of Hagar and Sarah, of Egypt and Canaan, bondage and freedom, Passover (kid) and Promised Land (milk). The destruction of our offspring is a sign that Israel has become another Egypt, a mother who, in an effort to usurp the authority of God, is unwilling to "let her people go." Israel's king has become another Pharaoh, a slave dealer (Jeremiah 34; Revelation 18:13).

Paul tells us in Galatians that Jesus, like Abraham, was choosing wisely between two mothers, between Old Israel and New Israel. As the Old Creation groaned, His Gospel-sword cut the heart of every Jew and manifested the sons of God.

Revelation culminates in the description of two women, a bipolar Israel. In her pain, as her Veil was torn away for the last time, the true sons of God were commanded to "come out of her."

One woman was a shelter, a prostitute justified by faith. Like Athaliah, the other sat on a stolen throne, drinking the blood of her own offspring.

And in her was found the blood of prophets and of saints,
and of all who have been slain on [the Land].
(Revelation 18:24)

In this shedding of immaturity, in obedience to the Covenant, Man is to outdo both tree and serpent.

31

Seed, flesh & skin

THE FRUIT OF RIGHTEOUSNESS

When you come into the land, and have planted all kinds of trees for food, then you shall count their fruit as uncircumcised. Three years it shall be as uncircumcised to you. It shall not be eaten. But in the fourth year all its fruit shall be holy, a praise to the Lord. And in the fifth year you may eat its fruit, that it may yield to you its increase: I am the Lord your God. (Leviticus 19:23-25 NKJV)

FOR MANY SKEPTICS, a strange command like this exposes an invented, self-contradicting and capricious god. In reality, moderns are brute beasts when it comes to the true nature of Creation. It is *sacrificial*.

Even Bible commentators don't often see beyond the fact that the early fruits of a tree are bitter and small. Keil and Delitzch, however, understand that this command concerning new fruit in the Land is Covenantal:

The reason for this command is not to be sought for in the fact, that in the first three years fruit-trees bear only a little fruit, and that somewhat insipid, and that if the blossom or fruit is broken off the first year, the trees will bear all the more plentifully afterwards, though this end would no doubt be thereby attained; but it rests rather upon ethical grounds.[1]

The Land of Canaan belonged to Israel by Covenant. This command concerning fruit from new plantings was instructive, just like the one in Eden. Israelites were to understand that trees were images of men (Mark 8:24). They were being transplanted into the Land as Adam was placed in the Garden. God desired the fruits of righteousness, under the cultivation of the Law, just as He did with Adam. So this command was both practical and ethical.

What is "uncircumcised" fruit? The ESV renders the word as "forbidden," which obscures the Covenantal intent of the directive. It is one thing to treat new fruit as inedible but quite another to consider it as a foreskin!—unless, of course, we consider fruit as a symbol of Man just as we considered animal sacrifices to be so.[2]

1   Keil and Delitzsch, *Biblical Commentary on the Old Testament.*
2   After reading this chapter, Steven Opp commented, "The idea of uncircumcised fruit helps make sense of the notion that Eve was being 'seduced' by the devil, allowing the uncircumcision to come into her, with its seed. It also supports the suggestion that Jesus was the fruit being put back on the tree. Along with being the serpent on the pole, serpents always being the picture of uncircumcision, he was the uncircumcised fruit on the tree, where he was cut off, circumcised."

Like Man, fruit has a seed, flesh and skin. Hidden inside, there are "tablets" containing the Law of the Fruit, the information required for abundance. The flesh surrounding and protecting them is designed to pass away, either rotting or giving life to birds, beasts and Man. Fruit is not naked but covered, robed in glory—*already complete*—a glory which attracted the eye of Eve. The skin is a public testimony.

Tying the triune structure of fruit to the investiture of Man in the Garden reveals the same ethical pattern in all Creation. The "first skin" is to be considered as nakedness, as "uncovering." It is not inherently sinful but turns into rebellion when we resist a call to greater glory. Putting off the flesh allows God to provide a greater, more glorious covering. After obedience, Adam was intended to be clothed in righteousness. The natural would be clothed with the spiritual. The temporary flesh, "eaten by God's Law," would be given back eternal. We see this reflected in the fact that each Israelite male was circumcised, but all Israelites were to wear a robe with tassels to remind them of God's Law. We see this in the fact that under the Law of Moses, plagued skin that revealed the flesh was unclean, yet once completely white it was "holy." As with Naaman the Syrian, an obedient "peeling" led to a better skin. Even in this shedding of immaturity, in obedience to the Covenant, Man is to outdo both tree and serpent.

Leviticus 19:23-25 even has a Covenantal shape. By describing the intent of the Israelite farmers, the first stanza prefigures in miniature the shape of the whole.

> When you *(Light - Sabbath)*
>   come into *(Waters - Passover)*
>   the land, *(Land - Firstfruits)*
>   and have planted *(Rulers - Pentecost)*
>   all kinds *(Swarms - Trumpets)*
>   of trees *(Mediators - Atonement)*
> for food, *(Rest - Booths)*

You can see both the Creation week (see p. 12) and Israel's annual feasts (see p. 13) reflected in this single sentence.

Here, the farmers were just like God planting trees in the Garden. It seems strange that fruit from the old trees planted by Canaanites was *not* to be considered uncircumcised and yet fruit from these new trees *was*. The answer is that mature, fruitful trees are all Israelites! They have been cultivated and God is pleased with the result.[3]

Now, we can see this pattern in the entire passage and make some observations by corresponding the microcosm of the first stanza with the macrocosm of the complete command.

---

3   The oak trees planted by Abraham would have been enormous by the time Israel took possession of Canaan.

226

Seed, flesh and skin

TRANSCENDENCE
Sabbath - "When you come into the land, and have planted all kinds of trees for food,
(Genesis - Creation)

HIERARCHY
Passover - then you shall count their fruit as uncircumcised. *(Exodus - Division)*

ETHICS GIVEN
Firstfruits - **Three years** it shall be as uncircumcised to you. *(Leviticus - Ascension)* It shall not be eaten.

ETHICS OPENED
Pentecost - But in the **fourth year** all its fruit shall be holy, a praise to the Lord. *(Numbers - Testing)*

ETHICS RECEIVED
Trumpets - And in the **fifth year** you may eat its fruit, *(Deuteronomy - Maturity)*

SANCTIONS
Atonement - that it may yield to you its increase: *(Joshua - Conquest)*

SUCCESSION
Booths - I am the Lord your God."
(Judges - Glorification)

The first cycle is revealed as a miniature Genesis, and we see the "firstborn" of the tree under the sword at Exodus. Leviticus gives us an Altar and a forbidden Table.

The fruit of the fourth year was a "firstfruits meal" for God and His priests. The sacrifice of their first mature fruit would allow God to pour out a "Pentecost," a greater harvest, upon each tree. Then we have the fruit given a new name, a sacrifice transformed from bloody Moriah to shiny Zion, from external Law to internal Law, from skinny "blood" to tasty "praise." The trees had become "bridal" in nature and would be granted *Succession*.

Israel is granted the fruit of the Covenant as the Ethics "received." The Covenant vow is taste and tongue. This allows God to pour out the blessing at *Sanctions*. The obedient "head" gives abundance to the harvest "body."

This peculiar little passage not only reflects the great themes of the Bible, it supports the idea that the prohibition upon the Tree of Knowledge in Eden was only temporary. In Israel's "liturgical farming" we see each new tree mature from priest to king. In bearing godly fruit, every tree was a prophet in Israel. When God came looking for fruit, He would be pleased to find more than fig leaves (Genesis 3:7; Mark 11:12-14) and the curse would be broken. He would discover the right kinds of seed, flesh and skin—an Israelite indeed (John 1:47-49; Hebrews 12:11).

Jesus' blood
covered the
believers, but we
must never forget
that His blood
was also avenged
upon those who
refused to believe.

32
Half the blood

BEHOLD, I MAKE ALL THINGS BLOODY

"Do not forgive them, Father.
They know exactly what they are doing."

THROUGHOUT THE BIBLE THERE ARE TWO DOORS, or more correctly, a door *and a window.*

Both of them involve blood. The first takes us out of the world (Passover/Red Sea); the second puts us into government (Jordan/Atonement). The first is the Egyptian door, the second is a window in Jericho. One mirrors the other chiastically in the journey from slavery to Sabbath.

Both of these doors involve children. The children in a faithful household were covered at Passover. The other children were slain. Those in Rahab's house were covered at "Atonement," but every man, woman, child and animal was slaughtered in the bloodbath at Jericho—under God's express command.

Being a preterist, I tend to major on the negative

things we find in the New Testament that mistakenly get applied to the entire Church age, and attempt to compensate for this error. In context, these negative things *do* apply to that "adulterous" generation, but blogger Halden Doerge picks up on the *positive* side of the two-edged curse.

> In the account of the passion in Matthew, the crowd responds to Pilate's declaration of innocence with the cry "His blood be on us and on our children!" (Matthew 27:25). A curious irony is found here. In that the people here are taking on the responsibility for Christ's death but do so in language that seems utterly Passoverish. And indeed, as it turns out Christ's blood will be "on" them and their children. Just as the blood of the Passover lamb protected the families of Israel in Egypt from the angel of death, so also Christ's blood will protect and save the very ones who shed it without regard for him.
>
> But it doesn't stop there. With the giving of the Spirit at Pentecost and the attending proclamation of the gospel of the resurrection, Peter claims that "This promise is for you and your children" (Acts 2:39).
>
> Here we see the ironic and futile nature of our resistance to Christ and the radical superabundance of God's self-giving in response to our hatred and violence. We go out for blood, thoughtlessly throwing our children in with us. God responds to us by coming to us again, as our victim, with words of forgiveness and promise.

Where we would condemn ourselves and our children, God continues to come again to us with promise, with the Spirit, with new, vivifying life.[1]

At Pentecost, many Jews were cut to the heart. They realized they had crucified the Lord of glory. They did not know what they were doing. They had been led astray, and like the woman caught in adultery, they were forgiven.

This is the half of the picture I missed, but *it is still only half the picture*. It is only the first door, the Veil of *Passover*. That's about the Covenant Head, Christ. It ignores the second door/window: the Laver of *Atonement*. This is about the Covenant Body, the Church. The sin of those who refused to join Her was high-handed. Like those who accused the woman caught in adultery, they knew *exactly* what they were doing. As James Jordan says, Jesus forgave Israel's unwitting crime against Him, but their deliberate crimes against His bride He would not forgive. This brings us to the two-edged nature of Atonement.

Doerge sees the fulfillment of Israel's feasts in the history of the first century Church, but we must not leave it after *Passover* and *Pentecost*. The apostles summoned a new Jew/Gentile "body" as *Trumpets*, and pronounced plagues against all those who would not obey the gospel.

1   Halden Doerge, *Us and Our Children*, www.inhabitatiodei.com

Atonement, the Day of Coverings, followed hard on the heels of Trumpets. It was the day that the Covenant *Sanctions* were poured out, the blessings *and* the curses. That is why there were two goats slaughtered on this day. The Great Day of the Lord came with the slaughter of the blessed saints as the first goat—the scarlet cord (Joshua 2:18)—and the destruction of cursed Jerusalem as the second. Herod's city was the Church's Jericho. The death of Jerusalem was a window through which the completed Old Covenant Church had to pass before its final end.

Flavius Josephus, in his account of the Jewish war, records that a cloister collapsed during the destruction of the city, killing six thousand women and children in one fell swoop. And Revelation shows the massacred saints, Old Covenant fruit and New Covenant firstfruits, rejoicing over this event. Jesus' blood covered the believers, but we must never forget that His blood was also avenged upon those who refused to believe—and their children.

> Because I have cleansed you, and you were not cleansed,
> you will not be cleansed of your filthiness anymore, till
> I have caused My fury to rest upon you. (Ezekiel 24:13)

So, the blood of Christ was upon the children of Israel in two different ways. Whether it was a blessing or a curse depended upon faith in Christ. Is it any wonder the condemned Jesus told the women who were weeping for

Him to weep instead for their children? This is the other half of the picture, the other edge of the liberating curse.

Interestingly, this entire process is prefigured in Exodus 24, near the beginning of the Mosaic age, when Israel submitted to the Law for better or for worse:

TRANSCENDENCE
Sabbath - The call to climb the **mountain** and worship from afar

HIERARCHY
Passover - Moses and the elders are **set apart**

ETHICS
Firstfruits - Moses **alone** shall come near the Lord (a new Covenant Head)

Pentecost - Moses tells the people the **Laws** and the people agree to **obey** them

Trumpets - The altar and twelve pillars are **built** (a new city-Body)

SANCTIONS
Atonement - Half of the blood is **sprinkled** on the children of Israel

SUCCESSION
Booths - Moses and the elders **feast** before God in safety. The glory-cloud rests upon the mountain

Israel worked in God's Garden and served in God's kitchen, at the gate of the heavenly court. Consequently, hers is a long history of meat and vegetables, Abels and Cains.

33

Recipe for disaster

READING THE BIBLE
WITH COVENANT EYES

What more was there to do for my vineyard,
that I have not done in it?
When I looked for it to yield grapes,
why did it yield wild grapes?
(Isaiah 5:4)

SINCE THE ACT OF EATING HAS A COVENANTAL SHAPE, there
are two questions we must ask. Firstly, what does eating
have to say about the Covenant? Secondly, what does the
Covenant have to say about eating? (Of course, we could
ask the same questions about the Covenant and sex.)

This approach is the answer to interpreting many of the
strange "sign" stories in the Old Testament. Each has a
Covenantal shape, including the account of Elisha purifying the deadly stew in 2 Kings 4:38-41.

GOD'S KITCHEN

TRANSCENDENCE

Sabbath - And Elisha came again to Gilgal when there was a famine in the land.

HIERARCHY

Passover - And as the sons of the prophets were sitting before him, he said to his servant, "Set on the large pot, and boil stew for the sons of the prophets."

ETHICS

Firstfruits - One of them went out into the field to gather herbs, and found a wild vine and gathered from it his lap full of wild gourds,

> *Pentecost* - and came and cut them up into the pot of stew, *not knowing what they were.*

Trumpets - And they poured out some for the men to eat. But while they were eating of the stew, they cried out, "O man of God, there is death in the pot!" And they could not eat it.

SANCTIONS

Atonement - He said, "Then bring flour." And he threw it into the pot and said, "Pour some out for the men, that they may eat."

SUCCESSION

Booths - And there was no harm in the pot.

Israel worked in God's Garden and served in God's kitchen, at the gate of the heavenly court. Consequently, hers is a long history of meat and vegetables, Abels and Cains. The firstfruits of the womb (animal or monetary substitutes) and the firstfruits of the Land were offered for the sake of greater blessings. However, these were not simply to be offered, but *prepared* and offered.

The sin of Israel's priesthood under the later kings was offering the firstfruits without preparing their hearts. The wild gourds here are symbols of the Gentile gods which had captured their hearts and blinded their eyes. As Peter Leithart observes, "Yahweh had given Israel a living, fruitful land, flowing with milk and honey and watered by rain from heaven, but idols make the land deadly."[1]

The account not only has a Covenantal shape, it is part of a greater Covenantal structure, in which this story seems to appear as *Atonement.* The remedy for the poison of the "wild" Cainite ingredient was an act of sacrifice, of pure flour, the offering of an Abel as firstfruits. The selfless death of a priest would not only save Israel but also render the Gentile kingdoms acceptable to God.

Every Bible text is self-effacing: it points to something else. This is the very nature of the Trinity, so it makes sense that we must read the Bible with Covenant eyes.

1   Peter J. Leithart, *1 & 2 Kings, Brazos Theological Commentary on the Bible,* p. 186.

Every believer is now expected to learn to feed himself. This is a glorious, albeit at times messy, process.

34

No more spoon-feeding

A PRIESTHOOD OF ALL BELIEVERS CAN BE MESSY

"If you've ever been to a Synod, you'll quickly find out that 'truth' is determined by numbers."

So remarked a Catholic contributor on a Protestant forum. Is this a fair criticism of Protestant disunity? How should Protestants reply? Thanks to James Jordan's teaching, I think I can offer an answer.

One of the greatest themes of the Bible is of growth to maturity. The Old Testament priesthood was about simply obeying the rules. Priests didn't have to think, just obey. The zenith of this period gave us Solomon's understanding, his wise reflections upon the Law.

After the captivity, applying God's Law in new situations and under new conditions (Gentile emperors)

241

required a greater degree of wisdom. Not only did scattering Israel enlarge the mediator-nation's sphere of influence, it was a move from the simplicity of priestly "bread-making" (follow the rules) to the tricky process of kingly "wine making," that is, *tough decisions.* This culminated in the Last Supper, when men were finally invited to drink wine before God as kings.

The New Testament caps the Old, but it continues the progress of maturity for God's people by giving us less-detailed instructions. Not everything is spelled out for us in the New Testament. We are commanded to ask God for the wisdom of Christ, our Greater Solomon.

Now, the Roman Catholic Church creates an earthly unity through its central system of doctrine (and I would argue that this is unity in error), but the Protestant system is a brave application of the biblical process of maturity. We have to work things out under new conditions, and in many situations which would have been unimaginable to previous generations of Christians.

This Roman Catholic preference for the security of "childhood" is perhaps the reason Catholics were denied wine at Mass, and congregational participation was kept to a minimum. These characteristics were the result of an Old Covenant approach to worship—the exclusivity of a central authority on earth and a priesthood limited to only certain believers.

The New Covenant gives us freedom because we are to be governed by the Spirit. We have the Law of Christ *within* us. The Roman Catholic Church legislated against such freedom in its fight against error, but this is not the way of God. It led to the obfuscation of the Scriptures, the quenching of the Spirit, and the institutionalization of error. Yet, the Roman Church is not alone in its fear of New Covenant freedom.

The Westminster Confession is treated by some as a sort of "paper Pope" for Protestants. That is, it holds, in practice if not in deliberate intent, an earthly authority over the Scriptures.

Concerning confessionalism, Peter Leithart writes:

...essential as the past is, for Protestants the past ought never become an ultimate standard. Even the fixed points can be freshly formulated (cf. recent developments in Trinitarian theology and in Pauline studies). Beyond those few fixed points, much remains up in the air (for Catholics and Orthodox too), and will for centuries to come, as Christians continue to pore over the Scriptures and seek unity of mind concerning what they teach. Scripture remains fixed and immovable, the test and touchstone always of everything. Our understanding doesn't stay fixed. Protestants should be perfectly comfortable with that.[1]

1   Peter J. Leithart, *Who's Got The Gateway Drug?*, www.leithart.com

We don't like the idea of trusting God with God's business. We want control. Seizing control is desiring kingdom—the fruit of the second tree—before God's time. The Bible shows us that this is what is behind every turn to the dark side in the history of Church and State. It is a lack of submission to the Word and Spirit of God.

The Spirit gathered the Church by the Scriptures, and the Church gathered the Scriptures by the Spirit. We are on the right track as long as we have biblical horizons.

The installation of a pope, whether in flesh or on paper, is a demonstrated lack of faith in Christ and a refusal to rely upon His authority to deal with our dilemmas case-by-case. It is a desire for a certainty in the particulars that we cannot have (at least not for now) and it will always lead the Church into error. As with the Oral Law of the Jews, the human additions to the fixed words of God end up subverting and usurping them. We can have no doubt that treating any confession as if it were inerrant will have a similar result over time, more or less.

This is the New Covenant, and we are required to think. The time of spoon-feeding is over, and every believer is now expected to learn to feed himself, and judge wisely. This is a glorious, albeit at times messy, process.

In the toolbox of
Creation, alcohol
is a powersaw.

35

Counterfeit virtue

THE ABANDONMENT
OF SELF-LEGISLATION

The Son of Man

  has come

    eating and drinking,

    and you say,

      'Look,

      a glutton and a winebibber,

    a friend

  of tax collectors and sinners!' (Luke 7:34)

SOME HELPFUL THOUGHTS CONCERNING ALCOHOL from my friend André Rook, with comments from me at the end:

> Alcohol is synonymous with sin for many. Still for others it is considered an act of Christian love to perpetually abstain from alcohol, to provide a good Christian witness to others. My beef with the latter view (the

247

former being easily dismissed on account of Scripture, and also condemned in the heresy of Manicheism) is that it creates a counterfeit virtue for the Christian.

The erroneous logic is as follows: 1. Alcohol itself is not inherently bad. 2. Perpetual abstinence from "stumbling" consumables is commanded from Scripture for reason of providing a good Christian witness. 3. Therefore, perpetual abstinence from alcohol is not bad; it is in fact a virtue.

My claim is that perpetual abstinence from alcohol is not good, and Scripture by no means condones this false conviction; it is in fact a counterfeit virtue.

Starting from the first premise: alcohol is not inherently bad. The positive of this negative statement is that alcohol is inherently good. Alcohol, being a creation of our Lord, is *intrinsically* good. Unlike the Manichees who understood evil to be tangible, Jesus states that 'it is not what enters into the mouth that defiles the man, but what proceeds out of the mouth, this defiles the man' (Matthew 15:11). Evil is not tangible; evil is spiritual. The Bible makes this absolutely clear (Genesis 1:11-12, Matthew 15:11, Romans 14:14, 1 Timothy 4:3).

The second premise is where things have gotten hairy in many modern churches; this is where my disagreement lies. In Kenneth L. Gentry Jr.'s book, *God Gave Wine,* he devotes an entire chapter to the exegesis of Romans 14. In that chapter, Paul is speaking to the Romans about the doctrine of Christian liberty. There were a few things that stuck out to me in this chapter.

One such point is the term "stumbling block" that many Christians like to throw around. What does this cryptic saying mean? What constitutes as a "stumbling block?" Gentry defines the Greek word used here: *proskomma*. As it turns out, this Greek word does not simply mean something that causes someone to feel uncomfortable or irritated. The meaning is much stronger than that. *Proskomma* in the Greek refers to something that causes someone to fall into sin against God. Notice the word "cause." If the effect of my cause is rebellion against the Lord, then I should not do what is in question. On how many occasions is moderate alcohol consumption a cause for sin? Let us answer the question with care, for our Savior Himself consumed alcohol in public, around the society's lowest, those most likely to be tempted with the sin of drunkenness.

The fact is that Christ did not cause anyone to sin. "Cause" implies intent. If it is my intent to cause someone to fall into sin, then I have sinned; I am responsible. We cannot *cause* someone to sin if it is not our intent to do so. If our intent is not to make others sin and simply enjoy God's goodness and providence, then the responsibility *literally* does not lie with us for the sin they may commit as the result of our lawful activity. We cannot unknowingly cause someone to sin, according to the very nature and definition of the word *proskomma*.

So how, then, should we approach alcohol? In the same way we approach everything else. With sobriety of mind and spirit, and with praise for our Lord on our lips. He is good, and all that He has created is good. Alcohol abstention is, in fact, nothing more than a counterfeit virtue, a "virtue" that Christ Himself did not practice.

It is dangerous business indeed to try and be holier than Christ; that was the Pharisees' fatal game. Let us give thanks to our Maker for the good things he has given to us to enjoy; let us praise Him by enjoying alcohol as He meant for it to be enjoyed. Cheers!"[1]

As C. S. Lewis has observed, Satan has only the materials that God created to tempt us with. Sin is an inappropriate use of good things—including other people. Everything has its place, and many things can be quite deadly if they are out of place. Internal bleeding or a punctured bowel are perfect examples. Greasy fried chicken is a blessing in moderation. Fried chicken grease from kids' fingers on your new leather lounge is not. Farming, mining, fishing and foresting are good. All of these in the extreme are bad. In all cases, we are called to use the created order justly, in faith, and with wisdom.

Just as bread is a symbol of priestly obedience (just follows the baking rules), wine is a symbol of wisdom. It is for someone who knows the rules and doesn't need them enforced. It is self-legislation, self-government.

1 Andre Rook, *Counterfeit Virtue,* http://drerook.blogspot.com

In the toolbox of Creation, alcohol is a powersaw: to be used wisely; not to be toyed with. "In the end it bites like a serpent and stings like an adder." (Proverbs 23:31-35).

As a picture of the Covenant cup, it brings both blessings and curses depending upon obedience. We experience the *shalom* of the kingdom, ruling over our enemies as Solomon, or we stagger and fall prey to those same enemies, as the kings eventually did. Jesus drank wine as a king, and He also drank the cup of Covenant curses at the Father's hand.

There is no disputing the tragedies that alcohol abuse continues to cause in many lives and families, experienced firsthand by many friends and acquaintances. For sure, those who cannot handle it should abstain—this was the sin of Adam. But is prohibition a wise decree—or is it a refusal to accept the role of government of the kingdom Christ has purchased and delegated to us? Wine is a call to maturity, a call to handle the serpent like a staff.

Even after his failure, the Lord called Adam to judge rightly. It appears He offered wisdom to Adam *again!* As with wine, the Tree of Knowledge was not inherently bad. It was the power tool required for dominion.

Reaching a maturity in judgment is always messy. The brave process of the historic synods, like child-rearing, is a risky one. It takes obedience. It takes faith in a God who promised the eventual glorious outcome from the beginning. But the *goal* is not obedience or faith (the Law written on our hearts). The goal is mediatory *wisdom,* the riches of discernment.

So a prohibition of alcohol is the same as a ban on farming, mining, fishing and foresting. It is a refusal to grow up and enter into government, the ministry of glorifying the world, and to take the risks this always involves.

This was the sin of the Pharisees, who preferred the dead, inflexible security of legal minutiae to the living, flexible, mature wisdom of One who was greater than Solomon. Because they would not drink with Christ, judgment was poured out upon them.

Boisterous with wine

Peter Leithart, commenting on
Zechariah 9:15, writes:

"In this context of warfare and triumph,
food and drink play an important role.
Yahweh's people, His weapons, would
'devour' their enemies, drink wine, and
become boisterous—as filled with wine
as the basin at the foot of the altar was
filled with blood, filled with wine like
the blood-caked 'corners of the altar'
(9:15). What Israel would find exhilarating was partly the 'wine-blood' of
her enemies, who had been slaughtered
before her. But the passage pictures
Israel drunk with another kind of wine:
filled with the wine of Yahweh's Spirit,
Israel would be bold, wild, untamed,
boisterous in battle.

This suggests one dimension of the symbolism of wine in the Lord's Supper: it loosens our inhibitions so that we will fight the Lord's battles in a kind of drunken frenzy. If this sounds impious, how much more Psalm 78:65, where the Divine Warrior Himself is described as a mighty man overcome with wine? Yahweh fights like Samson, but far more ferociously than Samson. He fights like a drunken Samson! Grape juice, it must be said, simply does not carry the same punch. Deprived of wine at the Lord's table, it is no wonder that we fight our battles so timidly, no wonder we stay so nerdy and are constantly plagued by bullies."

— Peter J. Leithart, *Blessed Are The Hungry*, pp. 110-111.

Pharaoh will feed divine meals to his gods, and then flay the Hebrews. Caesar will cut goats' gizzards, and then torch Christians. This is power religion. The faces of these gods are permanently hidden.

36

Incantation and incarnation

THE ART OF NOISE

But someone will say, "You have faith and I have works."
Show me your faith apart from your works, and I will show
you my faith by my works. (James 2:18)

THE FIRMAMENT WAS A VEIL TO HIDE GOD'S THRONE from
Man until he was ready to see God face to face. Of course,
we see types of this throughout the Bible. Job, Jacob and
Moses are notable examples of men who "saw the face of
God" in various preliminary ways. But no man could
truly see God until after Christ ascended and was
presented as "Facebread."

Your face is a veil of flesh that hides your brain, the
source of your intentions. Your head is a microcosm of
the Tabernacle at one level, and your entire body at
another. You are a Garden and a Land in the World.

Deceivers mask their true intentions with facial expressions and body language. Some people can even pass a lie detector test. Between their true intentions and the flesh that is supposed to be communicating it, there is a deliberate disconnect. As in the Garden, it is the mind of a beast speaking with the eyes and mouth of a man.

Made in God's image, our words create or destroy. Christians understand this. Christian writings are a testimony to this. Christian publishing is crucial. The cultures that grew up around Israel and grow up around the Church are cultures of words and books, crosswords and blogs. But in God's economy, in the way He has made things, mere words are not enough. Words are swords. They are made to cut something, even when they are intended to build up and edify.

Politicians stand before us and speak about hope and change to no effect. But God's words, unlike the words of men, never return to Him empty. Why is this? As Doug Wilson says, smooth words create hard hearts, both in the Church and outside of it.

The difference between the words of God and the words of men is the difference between incantation and incarnation. Muslim calls to prayer are very often not read "live" but broadcast recordings. Yet these recorded words do change reality. People obey. *Creation.* They obey because there is also a sword. Bodies move to mosques.

Division. The words become incarnate. Hearts are cut because if they are not, *flesh will be.*

Christianity is similar, but it requires a godly mediator. It is God's messenger who is the cut one. The sword-Word must pass through him first as a willing sacrifice. He is displayed on the Altar. This is not the coercion of Islam but a bridal invitation. This is where theonomy[1] over-reaches its God-given intent and becomes instead the anger of man (James 1:19-20). God's Law is for God's people. We can fill the world with books, but if we are not a people "cut," the hope we share will be empty words. We might as well be an army of teleprompters. The Veil has to be opened, and this involves the tearing of the flesh.

The religion of the Herods and of Mohammed and of modern statism is power religion. It is a "synagogue of Satan," the sorcery of Jannes and Jambres, the sect of Saruman. It moves flesh by coercion. Many with a past in Satanism will tell you their lives became filled with and controlled by fear.

Flesh must be moved, but Saruman hides in his prayer tower, with his words and his books. He himself will not be touched. The cutter refuses to be cut. This is not mediation because the "veil of flesh" remains untorn.

1   "Theonomy," derived from the Greek words *theos* (God) and *nomos* (law), is the state of being governed by God or in accord with divine law.

Pharaoh will feed divine meals to his gods, and then flay the Hebrews. Caesar will cut goats' gizzards, and then torch Christians. This is power religion. The faces of these gods are permanently hidden because the mediators will not make themselves vulnerable. They will not be open doors.

Many of us Christians are guilty of this hiding and manipulating and coercing, at home, in church, in business, in politics. I certainly am. Power religion, like Saruman, like Satan, doesn't get out much. Too risky. Easier to pull strings, name-drop, work the room. The Veil stays closed.

Dominion religion is the fearless offering of our bodies as living sacrifices. Jesus offers Himself to us, and then we offer ourselves to the world. When any tribe or city starts killing God's people, it is almost a sure omen that conversions will follow. The Words of the martyrs (witnesses) never return void. They are carried on a firmament of flesh whose division exposes the emptiness of the world and its words and reveals the face of God.

Books and words are crucial, but they are no good hidden away. God needs them written on flesh as well as stone. "Spells and smells" can be wonderful in worship, but those words and clouds must leave the building as the Warrior Bride. We must be preaching, singing and chanting the Scriptures. If the worship stays indoors, our faith is only, as Oswald Chambers would put it, "sentimental." Sentiment is fine but it must lead to action. It is crucial that we get our worship right, but it doesn't bring the powers crashing down unless the singing soldiers are marching into a (possibly) bloody battle. Then God does His magic.

> And when they began to sing and praise, the Lord set an ambush against the men of Ammon, Moab, and Mount Seir, who had come against Judah, so that they were routed. For the men of Ammon and Moab rose against the inhabitants of Mount Seir, devoting them to destruction, and when they had made an end of the inhabitants of Seir, they all helped to destroy one another. (2 Chronicles 20:22-23)

Working backwards, the content of the originating "liturgy" is also crucial. Good works without the accompanying truth also fall flat. Instead of returned mail, they are an envelope that is addressed and stamped but empty. Ahasuerus always sends out his fastest horses with a bill that cannot be repealed.

The Word becomes incarnate in us. We are called to worship. We are cut to the heart. We go out with an invitation but also an ultimatum. Unbelievers' hearts will be cut because if they are not, their flesh will be. AD70 is testimony to that.

"Come, everyone who thirsts,
come to the waters;
and he who has no money,
come, buy and eat!

Come, buy wine and milk
without money and without price.

Why do you spend your money
for that which is not bread,
and your labor
for that which does not satisfy?

Listen diligently to me,
and eat what is good,
and delight yourselves in rich food."

(Isaiah 55:1-2)

Samson prefigures not so much the crucifixion of Christ, but the sufferings of Christ "filled up" in the Firstfruits Church.

37

The sun of righteousness

SAMSON'S NEW EYES

It was not that this man sinned, or his parents, but that the works of God might be displayed in him. (John 9:3)

ALL THE COVENANTS IN THE BIBLE are a process of promise and fulfillment. Day 3 is the Day of Promise. Day 7 is the Day of Fulfillment. On Day 3 we have grain and fruit plants. They are the promise of bread and wine at God's Sabbath table on Day 7.

The third elected judge was Deborah. Her name means "bee," a taste of kingdom honey. Her song calls for a warrior like the sun. The seventh elected judge was Samson—"Sunrise."

One theme of Day 7 is the Great Prophet, a man who has been tried and found faithful and included in the council of God. He has passed under the seven eyes of the

Law (Day 4) and is now God's Law incarnate, a lamb (bread and wine) with seven eyes.

But Samson, the fallen bridegroom, lost his eyes. He was put to work grinding grain in a mill. There's the bread. What was the wine? Samson's blood. The wine of Communion is a dose of death. It is a cup of judgment that deals with the past and opens the future.

Blind Samson, now humbled, became the flaming eyes of God among the Philistine rulers. In his death, like Christ, Samson put to an open shame the principalities and powers who had mocked him for sport. Samson, like Christ, was perfected through suffering.

But Samson's story is more about the bride. The death of the Nazirite prefigures not so much the crucifixion of Christ, but the sufferings of Christ "filled up" in the Firstfruits Church. The Jews were blinded that the Gentiles might believe. Those Jews who were provoked to jealousy and did believe were humbled in the wilderness, excluded from the heritage they had boasted in, the things Paul judged to be dung.

From the Revelation it seems that a remnant of converted Jews were slain in the besieged city before it fell. They were the true Nazirites, the Warrior Bride. They brought down the pillars of Herod's Temple and in death became the foundations of a *New* Jerusalem.

For the saints, Jesus' death as bread and wine was the promise of a greater rest into which they would enter. Like Samson's glorious hair, growing out of a bloodied Covenant head, their strength was made complete in weakness.

We are bidden to the forbidden feast, a table where bread and wine are not only served to us as priest-kings, but irretrievably mixed together inside us, nourishment and *shalom* united at last.

38

The forbidden feast

MELCHIZEDEK'S ORDER

MANY THEOLOGIANS WILL TELL YOU that the Old Testament
Scriptures have little to say about resurrection. Yet, these
texts scream about it constantly—if we have eyes to see.

Old Testament history is a series of types. The shape of
events in Bible history always prefigures events that were
yet to come. That is the nature of God's revelation. Once
we understand this, we can see pictures of death and
resurrection, over and over again, at both personal and
national levels, hidden in plain sight.[1]

This death-and-resurrection process involves a passing-
over and a passing-*through*. At *Pass-over,* the people of
God are separated from the nations. At *Pass-through*

---

1   See *Bible Matrix: An Introduction to the DNA of the Scriptures* and *Bible
     Matrix II: The Covenant Key,* for a visual blow-by-blow account of this
     death and resurrection process in Bible history.

(Atonement), that "middle wall" of partition comes down, and Israel is reunited with the nations.

Now, we see this "matrix" in every part and in the whole. This pattern takes us:

- from the original promise of the Land to Abraham (Abraham "passed-over" in a deep sleep) to the destruction of Egypt (the death of the firstborn as the Atonement for Pharaoh's massacre of Hebrew infants, while Israel "passed-through" the sea);

- from the destruction of Egypt (Israel "passed-over" behind their bloodied doors) to the destruction of Jericho (Israel "passing-through" the Jordan, and Rahab's red cord in the window);

- and, when these two halves are combined as Head and Body (patriarchs and nation), the pattern takes us from the *promise* of the Land to the *conquest* of the Land.[2]

This greater pattern gives us the complete picture. The fall of the walls of Jericho ended the covering sacrifice that Abram mediated over Canaan more than four hundred years before. The very structure of Genesis 15 lays out for us liturgically the exact pattern of this Canaan-to-Canaan history.

2 For relevant diagrams, see *Bible Matrix: An Introduction to the DNA of the Scriptures* pp. 41, 61, 93, 115.

So, like Adam and Eve, Israel and the Land were torn apart (in a deep sleep) and then reunited with a promise of an abundant future based on obedience. But despite the fact that Israel was now settled among the nations, Israelites were still set apart. The conquest of Canaan did not end circumcision. In fact, the conquest *reinstituted it.* Joshua was commanded to circumcise Israel a "second time." There is blood in the division and blood in the reunion. This points toward an even greater fulfillment of the promise to Abraham, a larger pattern, one that would even tear down the Jew-Gentile divide. In the greater scheme of things, the cutting of Adam's flesh into Jew and Gentile—like bread and wine—would not be reversed until the destruction of the Temple in AD70.

All this background brings us to Melchizedek, the High Priest of Salem, as an imposing set of bookends to the Abrahamic divide. Before the institution of circumcision, worship was not centralized. Worship of the true God was carried out by men like Noah, priest-kings of all nations. In fact, centralized worship was part of the sin at Babel. It was a gathering of nations around a lie.

To avoid another flood, God tore humanity into two— priestly nation and Gentile kings—like bread and wine. Abram's feast with Melchizedek was the last time the Messianic line would eat bread and wine together, before God, until Christ. From the circumcision of Abram, bread and wine became "holy," a "forbidden mixture."[3] Both were present in the Tabernacle, but the wine was always poured out as an offering. It was never consumed in the presence of God by the priests. Bread and wine, flesh and blood, were divided.[4]

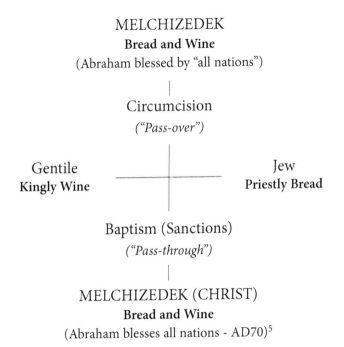

MELCHIZEDEK
Bread and Wine
(Abraham blessed by "all nations")

Circumcision
("Pass-over")

Gentile   Jew
Kingly Wine   **Priestly Bread**

Baptism (Sanctions)
("Pass-through")

MELCHIZEDEK (CHRIST)
Bread and Wine
(Abraham blesses all nations - AD70)[5]

---

3   For more on forbidden mixtures as "holy hybrids," see *Bible Matrix II: The Covenant Key,* chapter 8, "Elementary Things."

4   This is one of the evidences for Ezekiel's temple being fulfilled in Israel's history under Gentile kings before Christ. In that construct, the wine was still to be poured out for God, not consumed by men.

5   Notice that this five-step process follows the five-fold Covenant pattern, with the Mosaic "Ethics" as the dividing wall.

So Christ, as Melchizedek, serves the forbidden feast—bread and wine consumed together in the presence of God—to twelve men from the loins of Abraham. They are the representatives of a new, reunited body. He brings the Aaronic priesthood, the "division," to an end by allowing His own flesh and blood to be separated. "Pass-through" came with the destruction of centralized worship in Jerusalem. Abraham finally entered his heavenly country.

Old Covenant Israel was Adam broken and "tipped out." He was divided that he might be conquered. As with all the other forbidden mixtures in the Law of Moses, this recombination of bread and wine, Jew and Gentile, was holy, that is, impossible without the Spirit of God. The New Covenant Israel is Greater Eve, the marriage feast at God's Table.

The priests of God are no longer limited to humbling bread, and those to whom they minister as examples of kingdom citizens are no longer limited to the crumbs that fall off the table.

We are bidden to the forbidden feast, a table where bread and wine are not only served to us as priest-kings, but irretrievably mixed together inside us, nourishment and *shalom* united at last.

With holy bodies, we submit *ourselves* to be broken—divided—sacrifices—for the sake of world united by the New Covenant in the blood of Christ.

Animals can survive on food alone. Men also require a steady diet of truth.

39

Do not harm the oil & the wine

SALVATION THROUGH JUDGMENT

When he opened the fourth seal, I heard the voice of the fourth living creature say, "Come!" And I looked, and behold, a [green (Greek: chloros)] horse! And its rider's name was Death, and Hades followed him. And they were given authority over a fourth of the [Land], to kill with sword and with famine and with pestilence and by wild beasts of the [Land]. (Revelation 6:7-8)

THE FOUR HORSEMEN OF THE APOCALYPSE ARE THE GOSPEL. They were released as the first four seals on the New Covenant scroll were broken by Christ after His Ascension.

The white horse brings the Word, the red horse brings division (as Jesus promised), the black horse starves the old priestly order (the Old Covenant) but does no harm to the new. Finally, the green horse, an "emerald" Levite with a sword, brings the Old Covenant to an end by executing

275

the curses of the Law.[1] The Gospel itself puts "Israel according to the flesh" on the Altar. The final three seals concern the "Bridal Body" of Israel, a double-witness of Old and New Covenant martyrs, the Firstfruits of the Land. The seven seals herald a "new Creation."

Creation - The White Horse

Division - The Red Horse

Ascension - The Black Horse

Testing - The Green Horse (eye and tooth)

Maturity - The Unavenged Prophets

Atonement - Heaven and Earth Shaken

Glorification - Altar Fire from Heaven upon Earth

James Jordan notices that Revelation 7:15-17 also follows the Creation week pattern.

Light - Therefore they are before the throne of God, and serve him day and night in his temple;

Firmament - and he who sits on the throne will shelter them with his presence [under the "wings" of His robe]

---

[1] James Jordan observes that the colors of the horses allude to the gemstones on the breastplate of the High Priest. When Moses asked, "Who is on the Lord's side?" Levites came forth and slaughtered the idolaters. Ezekiel also witnessed "Levitical" angels sent to slay the wicked in Jerusalem. Jordan's lectures on Revelation are available from www.word.mp3.com

Land, Grain & Fruits - They shall hunger no more, neither thirst anymore; [New Covenant bread and wine]

Ruling Lights - the sun shall not strike them, nor any scorching heat [no more oppressive government from false shepherds]

Schools/Flocks - For the Lamb in the midst of the throne will be their shepherd, [the True Shepherd]

Man - and he will guide them to springs of living water, [a heavenly country]

Dominion - and God will wipe away every tear from their eyes. [Sabbath rest and clear judgment]

John refers to the sun-beaten, starving exiles in Isaiah 49:10. They were leaving captivity behind and seeking the liberty of a New Jerusalem. Here, however, the captives freed from the hypocrisy of the Pharisees were leaving Herod's Babylon hungry and thirsty *for righteousness*. Jesus saved the New Covenant "remnant" from the Apostolic "Levites" who, with their flaming swords (tongues), brought an end to the old order.

Though this text applies to the first century, the Gospel still unfolds in this fourfold pattern wherever it goes. It comes to free the captives and fill them continually with good things. Animals can survive on food alone but men also require a steady diet of truth. The truly hungry and thirsty are regulars at the Table of Oil and Wine.

Straight up

"The Reformation was a time when men went blind, staggering drunk because they had discovered, in the dusty basement of late medievalism, a whole cellarful of fifteen-hundred-year-old, two-hundred-proof grace—of bottle after bottle of pure distillate of Scripture, one sip of which would convince anyone that God saves us single-handedly. The word of the gospel—after all those centuries of trying to lift yourself into heaven by worrying about the perfection your bootstraps—suddenly turned out to be a flat announcement that the saved were home before they started... Grace has to be drunk straight: no water, no ice, and certainly no ginger ale; neither goodness, nor badness, nor flowers that bloom in the spring of super spirituality could be allowed to enter into the case."

— Robert Farrar Capon, *Between Noon and Three: Romance, Law, and the Outrage of Grace*, pp. 109-110.

The horn of plenty
marries the curse upon
Adam and the curse
upon Eve and unites
them as a blessing.

40

Being Cornucopia

THE TABLE IN THE MOUNTAIN

Truly, truly, I say to you,
unless a grain of wheat
falls into the earth
and dies,
it remains alone;
but if it dies,
it bears much fruit.
(John 12:24)

ISRAEL WAS GIVEN A "FIRSTFRUITS" TASTE of the Promised Land in Numbers 13. As with all Covenants, it was bittersweet. There were grapes, but there were giants. It was the same challenge as the one given to Adam. They were called to be judges who made their decisions based not on sight but on faith in the Word of their God.

God offers us a place at His Table, but between us and Him stands death's door. The Law must be satisfied before

He can pour out the Covenant blessings. Israel would inherit the crops and vineyards of Canaan but there would be bloodshed first. There is nothing inherently wrong with the fruit of Tree of Wisdom,[1] or Cainite fruit and vegetables, but the "fruit" of Adam, or the blood of Abel's offering, must come first. Priesthood precedes kingdom as the head precedes the body.

The traditional image of *cornucopia* is a perfect illustration of this process:

> The cornucopia (Latin: *Cornu Copiae*) is a symbol of food and abundance dating back to the 5th century BC, also referred to as the food of worship and holiness, Horn of Amalthea, harvest cone, and horn of plenty.
>
> In Greek mythology, Amalthea was a goat who raised Zeus on her breast milk, in a cave, on Mount Ida of Crete. Her horn was accidentally broken off by Zeus while playing together. The god Zeus, in remorse, gave her back her horn with supernatural powers, which would give whoever possessed it whatever they wished for. The original depictions were of the goat's horn filled with fruits and flowers: deities, especially Fortuna, were depicted with the horn of plenty. The cornucopia was also a symbol for a woman's fertility. The story is said to be a predecessor of the Unicorn and the Holy Grail stories.[2]

---

1 Judicial wisdom is the knowledge of good and evil.
2 From the Wikipedia entry for *Cornucopia*.

The relevance of fertility to the Covenant promises is obvious, but what is the significance of the horn? Horns are symbols of power. The very phrase "horn of plenty" contains the fruit of the head—the horn of Law—and the fruit of the body—the abundant outpouring of Grace. This image marries heaven and earth, death-and-resurrection. The horn of plenty marries the curse upon Adam and the curse upon Eve and unites them as a blessing.

Perhaps this explains the strange use of the "horn" in Isaiah 5. It's so strange that translators don't know what to do with it. Peter Leithart writes:

> Most translations say that the Beloved planted his vineyard on a "fertile hill," but Isaiah wrote that He planted it on "a horn, a son of oil" (Heb. *beqeren ben-shamen*). The phrase might refer to a fertile hill, but that's not what the words mean.
>
> The passage closest to Isaiah's usage is in Zechariah 4, where the two olive trees are called "sons of oil" (v. 14). In Zechariah, the phrase refers to Zerubbabel and Joshua, the two anointed ones who lead the post-exilic community. Zechariah doesn't use the word "horn," but it fits the context, since the anointed ones are anointed from horns filled with oil, and become the horns of Israel, the victorious wild ox.
>
> What would it mean to say that Yahweh had a vineyard on a "horn, a son of oil"? Verse 7 says that vineyard is "the house of Israel" and the men of Judah

are the "delightful plant" within the vineyard. That vineyard was planted "on" the anointed one, David and his descendants. The links are complex but fairly clear: David is anointed, hence a "son of oil"; Yahweh regularly raises David's horn on high; David is also a mountain "horn" on which Israel rests.[3]

Well, that is a good start, but it is only the exaltation of the Covenant Head. What about the Body? As in marriage, the "living sacrifice" of the Head is life to the Body.

Could the vineyard have been planted *in* the horn? Horns and anointing oil are generally concerned with the head. Horns, including those upon Israel's bronze and golden altars, were made to be bloodied, but only broken horns are bloodied with their own blood.

Joseph was exalted over his brothers, an exalted "horn," which his envious siblings subsequently broke. Yet, in his brokenness, Joseph brought abundance to Potiphar's household. Joseph was broken again, and prospered even in the stony barrenness of a prison. Finally, it was his chains that were broken and he was exalted once more, prospering Egypt and distributing the salvation of his abundance to all nations.

In Revelation 5, Christ was the Firstfruits Lamb. He poured out the olive oil of the Spirit at Pentecost and

3   Peter J. Leithart, *Son of Oil*, www.leithart.com See also Psalm 132:17.

sealed an entire army of sacrificial lambs, who are later pictured as grain and grapes. Through death, the Lamb emptied Himself and became a Holy Place, a Holy Land. The bloodied, emptied horn is followed by the Spirit, and the buried head brings a harvest. The Spirit overshadows the good soil and fills Him with bridal fruit.

That is also what we see in Zechariah. The cherubim that exiled Judah from the Garden-Land into the World have hammered their flaming swords into flaming plowshares. The result is a new burning bush, a multiplied Lampstand. With a renewed flow of Spirit oil, the Restoration era was a spiritual Cornucopia, despite outward appearances. When Jesus came to inspect it, the entire empire was ready for harvest. Enter Paul.

The same "horn of plenty" pattern was repeated in a grander scale in AD70. The Firstfruits Lamb was seen with seven new horns, seeking vengeance. As Jesus died for Judea, so all Judah (the kingly horn) would die for the abundant life of the world.

God is breaking wineskins that we hoped would last forever.

41

Out of the eater

A BIGGER CHRISTENDOM

"In the middle of its street,
and on either side of the river,
was tree of life,

which bore
twelve fruits,
each yielding
its fruit
every month.

The leaves of the tree
were for the healing
of the nations."

(Revelation 22:2 NKJV)

WHILE THE GOVERNMENTS OF THE FIRST GLOBAL ECONOMY in history struggle with challenges for which there are no historical precedents, Christians need to understand that even now, there is nothing new under the sun. It may be true, as some believe, that every war can be traced back to ethnic disputes over resources, but all the economic advice we need, whether personal, national or global, is contained in the Bible. The Tree of Life is still at the centre of the Garden. The source of all lasting prosperity is the Church, and God is growing her into a forest.

MATERIAL WORLD

Over the last century, the Church has suffered from a false dichotomy between the liberals and the fundamentalists; the materialists and the gnostics. R. C. Sproul Jr. writes:

Materialism and spiritualism breed on each other's extremes, fostering endless actions and reactions to each other. The great myth is that we must choose between them. However, we are not left to choose between these two distortions because Scripture offers a *tertium quid,* a third option, the notion that matter and spirit are both God's good creations, and therefore both good.

The Bible views the material world as the good creation of God. This judgment is more than the simple declaration that God saw it was good (Genesis 1). The Old Testament Jew viewed creation as a voluntary action of God. According to the Bible, the world did not evolve or emanate from some eternal substance. God chose to create it by divine fiat. The implication of this for the value of material things is staggering. God chose to create a material world. Within the framework of His own divine mind, he decided to make a world with food and drink and sex. Indeed he circumscribed the use of these physical things by His righteous law. He created them as good, included them in man's fall, and made them an integral part of man's redemption...

Redemption, in the full biblical sense of the word, is both physical and spiritual. The Bible does not divorce ministering to the physical and spiritual needs of people. The two may be distinguished but never separated. There is, to be sure, a difference between evangelism and a material welfare program, but they should go together.

Recent Christian history has witnessed an unnatural split between these two dimensions of Christian concern... [but] the biblical alternative assigns value to both the spiritual and the material. From Genesis to Revelation the God of Scripture holds out promises of material welfare. Abraham, by divine covenant pledge, was promised that his nation would receive land and property. He became one of the wealthiest men of antiquity, rivaled only by the patriarch Job. The exodus had profound economic overtones. God delivered a people oppressed as a slave-labor force, a people forced into destitute poverty...

The tabernacle and temple structures of the Old Testament were certainly not mere symbols. By divine instruction that included fine details, an exquisite structure was made for the sanctuary. [And the] items specified for the wilderness tabernacle pale in comparison with the splendors of the temple built in Jerusalem. The temple was an authentic wonder of the ancient world, its glory dwarfing even that of the cathedral of Notre Dame or Saint Peter's Basilica in Rome.

All these luxurious items were capable of abuse. Indeed, the judgment of God fell on the temple. Israel's silver became dross and its gold tarnished. But there remains a place for these things in God's kingdom. In themselves they are not to be despised. The biblical view assigns value to the body and the soul, to evangelism and social concern, to the spiritual and the material. Redemption is for the whole man.[1]

As a revived and refitted school of postmillennial optimism spreads, so must the Church's understanding of biblical economics as part of global redemption.

According to the *Bible Matrix,* the entire biblical history follows the pattern of the Tabernacle, which, in turn, is based on the Creation Week. The history of the Church is itself symbolically a construct of fine woods, gold and silver and precious stones, imported cloth, spices and incense (see Revelation 18). The Church is a temple made of people who have both spiritual and material needs, but its very means of growth is to minister out of

---

1   R. C. Sproul Jr., *Biblical Economics, A Commonsense Guide to Our Daily Bread,* pp. 29-37.

its abundance, both spiritual and material, not out of its poverty. It is not to our shame that the West is rich and other nations are poor. The economic state of every nation is evidence of the rule of the ascended Christ and His administration of Covenant *Sanctions:* the blessings and the curses. A visiting African pastor, amazed at Australian prosperity, commented that Westerners should stop feeling guilty about their wealth and start thanking God for it.

BECOMING THE TAIL

As a culture, the problem is not that the West has failed to minister out of its prosperity to non-Christian nations suffering from poverty or natural disasters. One cannot fault the heart of the West, a heart which wealthy non-Christian nations demonstrably do not possess.

The problem is that we have failed these nations by turning from the *source* of our prosperity, which is obedience to the New Covenant, the gospel of Christ. Following the example of Israel's kings, we deny the spiritual nature of our material malady. And worse, as our glory begins to tarnish and fade, we maintain an appearance of prosperity by exploiting the very nations we were called to serve.

Poverty and oppression always result from the abuse of Covenantal authority. As with the Babylonian captivity, there was a Covenantal reason for the oppression of the

Jews by Rome. After the captivity, Israel was restored for a more prophetic, advisory ministry for the nations. A godly Jew would be the right hand man of a Gentile emperor. But the Jews forgot this and once again demanded a Jewish king before time. God gave them the Herods, forgers of false covenants, masters of compromise. The Covenant blessing for obedience still applied:

> The LORD will open to you His good treasure, the heavens, to give the rain to your land in its season, and to bless all the work of your hand. You shall *lend* to many nations, but you shall not borrow. And the LORD will make you the head and not the tail; you shall be above only, and not be beneath, if you heed the commandments of the LORD your God, which I command you today, and are careful to observe them. (Deuteronomy 28:12-13)

And the Covenant curse for disobedience still applied:

> The alien who is among you shall rise higher and higher above you, and you shall come down lower and lower. He shall lend to you, but you shall not lend to him; he shall be the head, and you shall be the tail. (Deuteronomy 28:43)

Jesus' citation from Isaiah was offensive not because He claimed to be the Messiah, but because the text he read condemned His hearers for failing to keep the Restoration

Covenant. Instead of faithfully serving the nations (state) as a nation of priests (Church), and receiving the riches of the nations in return (as the Levites did in old Israel's Church-state), the Pharisees were *enslaving their own brethren* and further alienating the aliens. According to Moses, it was quite legal to charge usury of aliens, but not of fellow Israelites. Ezekiel's and Jesus' condemnations of usury were not condemning usury *per se.* These came within a Covenant context. Because the Jewish rulers had not been faithful with the talent they had been given, even what they had would be taken away.

The decline of the West is Covenantal. Christ is teaching "post-Christian" nations a similar lesson. Whether liberal or fundamental in our focus, our thinking is out of step with God. That is, we are either so heavenly-minded that we have retreated from the world, or so earthly-minded that our lawlessness disqualifies us from God's blessing. Thus, Jesus has made us borrowers instead of lenders. Because of our unbelief and disobedience, post-Christian nations, once the head, are becoming the tail.

NEW NINEVEH

...a time to kill, and a time to heal; a time to break down, and a time to build up... (Ecclesiastes 3:3)

The first century history followed the same pattern as God's previous dealings with Israel. When His people would not listen, He provoked them to jealousy. He raised up other nations, Assyria and Babylon, to teach them a lesson. He sent His prophets to those nations, and converted them! The ministries of Jonah, Elijah and Elisha were identical to that of Paul. They were *ministries of provocation.* God slew the old kingdom of *warriors* and resurrected it as a kingdom of *priests,* with a larger sphere of influence.

In this new world, the Jews were the spiritual head, and their synagogues sustained the empires and made them rich. When this order grew old, the Judaic head died for the body, and Christendom was the eventual result. This new kingdom was both spiritual and material, the "world to come" referred to by the writer of the book of Hebrews. As with "material and spiritual," Church and state are to remain distinct, but distinct as husband and wife. Christian society is the goal of the Church, the body for which the Church as head continually dies.

So, the resulting "West" has been the head, and Jesus is provoking it to jealousy, for the ultimate prosperity of all nations, a redemption that is both spiritual and material.

SOMETHING SWEET

If we believe the Bible at all, God is breaking wineskins that we hoped would last forever. The sequence of crisis, death and resurrection is His *modus operandi*. He is again shaking the Land to enlarge His house, stretch out His tent, build a bigger Christendom. The death of Western culture is merely the pruning of the Church. Any reconstruction begins with some deconstruction, some breaking down to build up, some humbling before exaltation. As James Jordan says in his book, *Crisis, Opportunity and the Christian Future,* we are living at one of the most exciting times in history.

The current global situation is another curve ball for the human race, another step in our growth to spiritual maturity and material prosperity. Christ rules all nations, and now all nations, through the ministry of the Church, will learn that sustainable prosperity only comes from the Man at the right hand of God.

> *Out of the eater came something to eat.*
> *Out of the strong came something sweet.*
> (Judges 14:14)

History is spiritual and material, an expanding lineage of heads and bodies. The microcosmic history of the Christ and His Firstfruits Church is being played out in ever-expanding macrocosms. The singular head dies for a multiplied body. The old kingdom dies so that a new one can be born. Inside the carcass of the kingly lion, whether Davidic Israel or Christendom Mark I, is a swarm, a new Bride. Even in its death throes, the beastly old West ministers the honey of Canaan to the world. And after the Church remembers, in her poverty, that spiritual riches come first, and Jesus invests her once again with authority and glorifies her with even greater plunder and delicacies, her envious critics will yet again be left to eat their words.

The real one per cent

"The Bible is not a history of poor people struggling under oppression. Nor does the Bible ever give any example of poor people rising up and overthrowing established order. Deliverance, when it comes, comes from people who are not poor helping those who are. The Bible history is a history of wealthy and royal people, giving us an example of how we are to think and live now that we are all wealthy and royal in Christ as members of His Kingdom Body."

— James B. Jordan, *Getting Real with the Patriarchs,*
Biblical Horizons No. 202.

In Peter's recommission, and in ours, there is a call to sacrificial life. There is a transfixing redness to the New Covenant dawn.

42

Breakfast at dawn

FEED MY LAMBS

And the Lord turned and looked at Peter. And Peter remembered the saying of the Lord, how he had said to him, "Before the rooster crows today, you will deny me three times." (Luke 22:61)

THE HOUSES OF WOOD AND STONE under the Old Covenant were always destined to become a temple of flesh. This is the reason why many of the prophetic visions which speak of architecture but have not found fulfillment in wood and stone are regarded by some as yet unfulfilled. But they *were* fulfilled—Head and Body—in Christ and in Spirit-filled men and women.

The ministry of Jesus follows the same blueprints as the ministry of Moses. He constructed a new house of worship before the old house was torn down. An understanding of Old Covenant architecture is essential to plumb the depths of the New Testament.

One of the most beautiful examples of this is the failure and recommission of Peter. In Peter, Jesus takes the people of Israel from outside the tent of Moses to sit inside as priests and elders.

Peter warmed himself at a fire outside the house of the High Priest. Architecturally, he stood at the **Bronze Altar.** The Covenant Ethics are three tests, symbolized in the blood, the fire and the smoke—or flesh, eyes and life.[1] When tested, Peter refused to identify himself with the Lamb.

Luke records that Jesus "looked" at Peter. Whenever Jesus "looks intently" in the Gospels, He is the **Lampstand,** the Law, the eyes of God, the watchman lifted up over Israel as sun, moon and stars. The lunar feasts were fast fading as the sun of righteousness arose. And the rooster heralded the dawn.

John records the dawning of a better day. This time the fire is not on the Land but by the Sea. The focus has shifted from the centre of Israel to her borders with the wild nations. The resurrected Jesus invites Peter not to offer himself to death but to dine with One who has

---

1   John uses the flesh, eyes and life to signify the Bronze Altar, Lampstand and Incense Altar in 1 John 2:15-17. See *Bible Matrix II: The Covenant Key,* p. 273. These also correspond to the three tests Jesus faced in the wilderness, and the three comments Eve made in her judgment of the fruit of the knowledge of good and evil.

conquered death on his behalf. Architecturally, Peter has passed through the Laver—from death to life—to join Christ as an elder at the **Altar of Incense**.

Again, Peter is tested three times. Instead of Altar; Fire; Altar, it is Feed; Tend; Feed. In this way, Jesus deals compassionately with past failure and calls Peter to a better future (as He does with us every week at the Lord's Table). But in Peter's recommission, and in ours, there is a call to *sacrificial* life. There is a transfixing redness to the New Covenant dawn.

The "official" death-and-resurrection of Peter would be repeated in the Firstfruits Church. When Jesus told Peter to feed His sheep, they both knew those sheep, like Peter, were being fattened for the altar.

Animal sacrifices were no longer acceptable now that Jesus had died and risen again.

But in Jesus, human ones were.

> *For whoever would save his life will lose it,*
> *but whoever loses his life for my sake*
> *and the gospel's will save it.* (Mark 8:35)

Godly conversations around the dinner table with your kids end up toppling godless empires.

43

The hidden power of Groundhog Day

or DOMINION BY STEALTH

I RECENTLY LISTENED TO A *WHITE HORSE INN* PODCAST, entitled *Boredom and Entertainment*.

> Compared with an action-packed movie, most people would probably characterize the ministry of the word and sacrament as "boring." So in order to reach out, should churches make their services more entertaining? Joining the panel for this discussion is Richard Winter, author of *Still Bored in a Culture of Entertainment*...

A story is told of children left in a room, each alone with a marshmallow on a plate. Each child was told that if he waited to eat it until his interviewer returned, he would receive an extra one. The kids who waited turned out to be more successful in every area of life. Both Winter and the panel, however, failed to connect this to the Garden of

Eden. The Sunday School teacher at our church made the connection straight away.

The panel does makes some keen observations. One is that this world and everything in it is designed to grow to maturity slowly. That is the way things are, so this modern compulsion to make everything "special" and "entertaining" consistently falls flat. We want glory and we want it now. But when Satan offers any shortcut to the kingdom, it is always a counterfeit of the real thing.

They relate this to youth groups which continually attempt to outdo the excitement of the last event with something more exhilarating and outrageous. It is noted that the youth ministries which are paring things back to basics and just studying the catechism (even Baptists!) have tripled their attendance because they are working with the grain of the created order instead of against it. This is the path to true greatness.

I hope your life isn't always like Groundhog Day, but to some extent, that is how life basically is. Daily life is a discipline that prepares us for eternity. Jordan notes that sleeping and waking, evening and morning, is a symbol of death and resurrection—*every day.*

Every day is a new opportunity for Dominion, and thus follows the pattern laid down in Genesis 1 (Creation), Exodus 25-31 (the Tabernacle), Leviticus 23 (Feasts) and in the Slavery to Sabbath narrative throughout the Bible

(Dominion). It is eating the elephant one bite at a time, reclaiming the Land from the Sea one day at a time.

> **Genesis** - You wake from sleep
> > **Exodus** - You go to work
> > > **Leviticus** - You are given instructions
> > > > **Numbers** - You work under instruction. Your faculties are tested
> > > > **Deuteronomy** - The work brings you prosperity and wisdom
> > > **Joshua** - You return home
> > **Judges** - You eat and rest

All this makes greater sense to me of some of King Solomon's statements in Ecclesiastes. He had experienced all that Israel's best youth pastors could thrill him with, but finally discovered the hidden, simple power in Groundhog Day.

> Go, eat your bread with joy, and drink your wine with a merry heart; for God has already accepted your works. Let your garments always be white, and let your head lack no oil. Live joyfully with the wife whom you love all the days of your vain life which He has given you under the sun, all your days of vanity; for that is your portion in life, and in the labor which you perform under the sun. (Ecclesiastes. 9:7-9 NKJV)

> Let us hear the conclusion of the whole matter: Fear God and keep His commandments, for this is man's all.

> For God will bring every work into judgment, including every secret thing, whether good or evil. (Ecclesiastes 12:13-14 NKJV)

Jesus is conquering the world not through political rallies, or even gospel ones; not through any dramatic action or newsworthy miracle. He turned Jacob's 70 into a nation over a quiet 400 years. He brought the Gentile empires to harvest time over another quiet 400 years (quiet at least as far as the Bible is concerned). He is slowly conquering the kingdoms of this world, and will continue to do so, until all His enemies are under His feet. It doesn't make the headlines, but every day, in every way, His kingdom is undermining, cracking, destroying and replacing this world like tree roots under a derelict building.

Every human day follows the heptamerous Covenant pattern. Every human day follows the Tabernacle pattern. Every day is thus an opportunity to measure out the heavenly blueprint upon the earth. This is what "Thy kingdom come" actually means. Maturity is understanding that small decisions echo in eternity; Godly conversations around the dinner table with your kids end up toppling godless empires.

Jesus knows the hidden power of Groundhog Day. It is humble, faithful perseverance in the small things, beginning with Word and Sacrament.

Renewing the vows

"...no first-century Jew would have failed to note a dramatic change in synagogue worship. Even though the pre-Christian synagogue services were modeled on the Temple liturgy, the one thing they could never do during their weekly services was partake of the sacrificial meals. One memorialized Yahweh and experienced Covenant renewal at the great feasting hall of the Temple.

In the new world, however, after the death and resurrection of Christ, the Church is the new Temple. She feasts with the King of Kings every week when she gathers. The fact that the Covenant renewal meal is an integral part of weekly Christian worship was a dramatic experience for the first-century Jews."

— Jeffrey J. Meyers, *The Lord's Service*, p. 58.

Even the most mundane chore is the history of the world hidden in a riddle.

44

Corpus Christi

THE JUDGMENT OF THIS WORLD

REGENERATION, PERSONALLY, CULTURALLY AND GLOBALLY, is a process. The Bible Matrix shows us that this process is echoed in all the activities of life. Even the most mundane chore is the history of the world hidden in a riddle. Sowing, farming, cooking, eating and cleaning are separate processes yet all part of the glorious work of life.

PRIESTLY FARMING (GARDEN)

So, whether you eat or drink, or whatever you do,
do all to the glory of God. (1 Corinthians 10:31)

Just as the instructions for the Levitical animal sacrifices hint at the "liturgical" significance of human body parts, so the correspondences of the various harvests with Israel's festal year open a window on the symbolic nature of "Edenic" grains and fruits. As we eat and drink Jesus, we appropriate centuries of God's labor in the land of Israel.

311

Sabbath - **Oil and Wine**
The outflow (Succession) of the
previous harvest year

Passover - **Unleavened Bread**
Israel's old history is cut off,
requiring new life by a miracle

Firstfruits - **Barley, Wheat and
Legumes**
Basic foods are given first, like
the Tree of Life, and the manna

Pentecost - **Grains and Seeds
(Sesame, Flax and Millet)**
Oil-bearing seeds carry
the Words of Life

Trumpets - **Grapes and Figs**
The promised fruits ripen as Israel's
troops are assembled

Atonement (Coverings) - **Pomegranates**
The High Priest's robe was hemmed with
alternating pomegranates and bells,
seed-and-bride, death-and-resurrection
(Exodus 28:35)[1]

Booths (Ingathering) - **Olives**
Israel, a holy nation once again, is a host to all
nations. The Spirit has been made flesh

1   The root word for the Hebrew "pomegranate" means "to lift up." It
seems to concern the Covenant Head (silence). The root word for the
Hebrew "bell" means "to impel." It concerns the Covenant Body
(music), driven by the Spirit.

312

Sabbath - The oil and wine are blessings from Israel's previous faithfulness. They symbolize her faithful priesthood and subsequent delegated kingdom. But the process must begin once again. Continued life comes by continued eating, which in turn comes by continued faith. Likewise, every year, the Covenant must be renewed.

Passover - Leaven symbolizes historical continuity. The old history has to be purged completely. Israel passes under the sword that she may be qualified to carry it.

Firstfruits - Basic grains are a body to be broken

Pentecost - The priestly body is anointed with legal (kingly) authority.

Trumpets - In response to her king, the abundant (fruitful) "bridal" body is prepared and robed.

Atonement - Pomegranates have a blood-red flesh and a bitter covering, but they are sweet to eat and produce beautiful flowers. They are the Bridal Couple righteous and united before God.

Booths - Gethsemane, the olive press, is the culmination of God's purposes for Israel. To be a blessing to all nations, she would die for the life of the world.

GOD'S KITCHEN

Kingly Dining (Land)

So I commended enjoyment, because a man has nothing
better under the sun than to eat, drink, and be merry...
(Ecclesiastes 8:15 NKJV)

Adam's faithful priesthood in the Garden would have led to a kingly role in the Land. The laborious process of farming leads to the two-edged process of cooking and eating. There is still labor involved but there is now a greater pleasure than simple satisfaction in a task. In our eating and drinking, we judge—*assess*—the world.

The farming year began during the Creation week, but only under Moses was it officially described as a succession of Divine feasts. Israel was freed from *slavery* and given a calendar of *holidays*. There was still labor involved but labors now led to godly pleasures. And, as every chore was a microcosm of Covenant history, so was every feast—and a feast was a promise of a better, more kingly, Covenant.

If you love the Bible, why not arrange a "Covenant banquet," a Divine Feast, according to the Bible's matrix, and explain Covenant history to your guests? After all, that was what Israel's feasts were supposed to do...

---

2   In Covenant history, this is the 24 angels in the Revelation carrying out their final Old Covenant tasks and leaving the Holy Place vacated for the saints. The Old Covenant servants leave the house to the New Covenant sons.

3   Based on a chiasm by my friend Albert Garlando.

A – **Invitation** (the Call)

    B – **Hospitality promised**
    (open door – DELEGATION/CLOSED VEIL)

        C – **Table setting by Host** *(forming)*
        (sacrifice of blood – BRONZE ALTAR)

        a – call of servants – *Fasting*

        b – table cloth
        (house robed – TABERNACLE)

        c – place setting / silence (Moses)

        d – candles

            D – **Cooking**
            (transformation – LAMPSTAND)

        C – **Table seating of Guests** *(filling)*
        (sacrifice of praise – INCENSE ALTAR)

        d – candles lit

        c – place seating / music (David)

        b – guests honored
        (if robed – TEMPLE)

        a – dismissal of servants – *Feasting*[2]

    B - **Hospitality enjoyed**
    (closed door – VINDICATION/OPEN VEIL)

A – **Rest** (and Rule)[3]

GOD'S KITCHEN

Prophetic Smoking (World)

Smoke went up from His nostrils, and devouring fire from his mouth; glowing coals flamed forth from him. (Psalm 18:8)

Prophets advise their king in the way Eve was designed to advise faithful Adam. Israel's age of kings was followed by a prophetic witness to the Gentile emperors, the "kings of kings." This "bridal" voice is an intuitive wisdom.

The process of maturity is reflected in the rite of sacrifice. After the blood of priesthood and the "ethical" fire of kingdom comes the "smoking firepot" of prophecy. Smoke is fragrant. Smoke is "bridal." When God's nostrils are kindled, it is because kings are oppressing widows and orphans: Greater Eve is being exploited.

And I will show wonders in the heavens and on the earth, blood and fire and columns of smoke. (Joel 2:30)

It is no coincidence that as the Incense Altar is central to the Tabernacle furnitures, so the nose is central to the face. Smoke is glory, and glory is death to the flesh. Smoking can kill you. However, it is telling that in tribal communities, smoking was communal (that is, corporate) and only occasional. It was related to eldership.

My friend Nathan Ketchen, an avid pipe smoker, has observed that the process of pipe smoking accords with the Lord's Service. It is tongue-in-cheek, yet illustrates a basic truth. Here is his seven-step "holy smoke" chiasm:

Creation - Place the tobacco in the pipe

Division - Pack the tobacco down tightly

Ascension - Place pipe in mouth

Testing - Light tobacco with fire from heaven

Maturity - Puff with mouth

Conquest - Pack down the tobacco some more

Glorification - Empty out the ashes when done

Notice the Lord putting the Law-pipe *into* Moses' mouth at *Ascension* (Leviticus, the Bronze Altar) and the smoke coming *out of* Moses' nostrils at *Maturity,* the second Law (Deuteronomy, the Incense Altar). Nathan's positioning of the firstfruits smoke (the martyrs) is absolute perfection. However, his pattern ends not with ingathering but with scattering, which is Babelic. Instead, I would suggest highlighting the corporate glory cloud at this point. The evening should end with a New Jerusalem.

The temple was filled with smoke from the glory of God and from His power... Revelation 15:8

THE BODY OF CHRIST

The feast of *Corpus Christi* celebrates the belief that the actual body and blood of Christ are present in the Eucharist. However, it would be more correct to say that, in our obedient remembrance, we *become* His body and blood, a festal invitation sealed and sent to the nations.

Smoke going up forever and ever...

"Beer drinking and pipe smoking will get you facedown and covered in ashes. But wouldn't you rather be remembered for your prayer life?"

We want *quick* judgments from the prophets, but instead He invites us to take our time and swill the delicate flavors of *every single variety* of grape in the Vineyard of Wrath.

45

Eschatology as cooking

As a young Christian, I found the New Testament irresistible and the Old Testament mysterious. But as I actually read through the Old Testament, I also discovered it could be really annoying. Instead of procuring snappy answers, sound bites and knockout quotes, there were long stretches of detailed information and seemingly redundant poetry. Surely Jeremiah and Lamentations could have been combined and slashed to a few short, sad chapters. Daniel *is* relatively short, but its second half has caused nothing but problems. Isaiah is inspiring in parts, but as tedious as "Question Time" in Parliament in many places. He should have just gotten to the point. After all, wasn't calf skin horrendously expensive?

Family devotions, church, Bible college and seminary would be far simpler, and way more efficient, had the

Lord employed the Reader's Digest editors before publishing. And He might have avoided the Marcionism of the modern Church, which, in practice if not in creed, regards the Old Testament as unnecessary and even dangerous.

Of course, the book of Revelation is treated in the same way, or worse. Verses and verses and verses of weird stuff. Why didn't Jesus just tell John to write a big sign, "CONDEMNED" and slap it onto the east gate of Herod's Temple? Much more efficient, surely. Luther wouldn't have doubted its canonicity; Christian publishing could have avoided suffering a lot of really poorly written fiction by Darby, Lindsey, LaHaye, Walvoord and Ice and the ridicule and confusion it brings upon the Church; and Messianic Jews would lose their air of superiority and have no excuse for not integrating fully with the Church.

As with cooking. when it comes to Church history, God is clearly not interested in simplicity. He is no minimalist. Yes, the Most Holy Place was a cube, but nothing else about the Tabernacle had the sleekness of Apple hardware. We moderns love clean click-wheel circles and neat nano squares but our God is more into fractals. He loves a decorated, cluttered house. This is reflected in His Word, and it is high time we turned back the clock, not to flowery Victoriana, but to the rich, symbolic understanding of the world enjoyed by the medievals and the ancients. Such ornament is not redundant. Sublimity *is* a function. Once we become accustomed to it, the Old Testament is an inexhaustible feast for the mind's eye, the poet's imagination, the musician's ear, the soldier's bottle, the lover's heart, and the saint's sustenance.

God's literary world is just like His Creation: a handful of relatively simple, raw, literary-mathematical formulae whipped together into an unfathomably complex delight. But we want a drive through burger instead of slow meditation on the Levitical laws. We want *quick* judgments from the prophets, but instead He invites us to take our time and swill the delicate flavors of *every single variety* of grape in the Vineyard of Wrath. We fill our little heads with thousands of three minute songs yet He invites us to let the slow symphony of Psalms wash over us again and again.

Of course, this apparent superfluity does attract boffins who write long-winded, boring commentaries on it full of circuitous footnotes. The systematic theologians are the dads at the theological party. Oblivious to the real glories the Bible, their *modus operandi* is to don lab coats, scoop the gravy off the lamb and put it in Tupperware. They disassemble the feast and weigh its separate elements. They incinerate the fat and count the kilojoules, all the while failing to be aroused by the aromatic glories of God's handiwork.

323

The Bible has to be rescued from such people. They do not understand the necessity for the Church of our God's literary excesses. Revelation comes as waves that alter the shoreline, courses that alter the waistline, so no expense is spared. Even the sorbets, Obadiah and Jude, have wondrous depths.

The artistry of the long-winded prophet is not an antiquated, culture-bound legalese. Certainly, their knives are sharp, but Isaiah, Jeremiah, Jesus and John carve up the body with the care of an accomplished chef, not the utility of a neighborhood butcher. They are masters of combining well-known ingredients in delightful new combinations.

By dining with the right people, we slowly develop a taste for literary structure and allusion, and we realize that the Scriptures are not a mind-numbing redundancy but an alluring, engaging, exquisite abundance, one that cries out to be savored and shared.

Either way, we are food...

"Your stew, so long deferred, stands finally *extra causas*. Greet it as your fellow creature. It is as deliciously unnecessary as you are."

— Robert Farrar Capon, *The Supper of the Lamb: A Culinary Reflection,* p. 98.

In one sense, we get our wings in the same way as *The Very Hungry Caterpillar* did.

46

Figures transfigured

HERE IS THE CHARMING PASSAGE quoted by Doug Wilson that led me to read *The Supper of the Lamb* by Robert Farrar Capon. It speaks of a kind of partying that is foreign to both the world and the modern Church. It is nothing like the pretense of joy offered by the world, yet such celebration is also alien to modern Christians. It is not sinful, yet it is so "incorrect" that it *must* be true.

> I wish you well. May your table be graced with lovely women and good men. May you drink well enough to drown the envy of youth in the satisfactions of maturity. May your men wear their weight with pride, secure in the knowledge that they have at last become considerable. May they rejoice that they will never again be taken for callow, black-haired boys. And your women? Ah! Women are like cheese strudels. When first baked, they are crisp and fresh on the outside, but the filling is unsettled and indigestible; in age, the crust may not be so lovely, but the filling comes at last into its own. May

you relish them indeed. May we all sit long enough for reserve to give way to ribaldry and for gallantry to grow upon us. May there be singing at the table before the night is done, and old, broad jokes to fling at the stars and tell them we are men... The road to Heaven does not run *from* the world but *through* it.[1]

What a delightful image! In one sense, we get our wings in the same way as *The Very Hungry Caterpillar* did. The Church should be known for its celebrations as much as for its sacrifices. Both are attractive. Both are holy.

To quote Douglas Adams, I think the real reason many Christian stuffed shirts disapprove of such gatherings is because *they* don't "get invited to those sorts of parties." *What winebibbers those Christians are!* The key is not to wait for an invitation. The key is to *throw* those sorts of parties. Sacrifice is the means to this end.

Yes, in the bigger picture, there is certainly a time for fasting. But our New Covenant feasting is also glorifying to God. In Esther, the "atonement" fast lasted for *one single day* and it resulted in the *permanent* two-day Feast of Purim. The sufferings of David led to the end of Saul and the regular feasts of Solomon's kingdom.

---

1 Robert Farrar Capon, *The Supper of the Lamb: A Culinary Reflection*, p. 180.

To use Luther's analogy, the trick is not to fall off either side of the horse, into glorified fasting or inglorious feasting.[2] Together, as work and rest, means and end, there is the perfect marriage of thrift and largesse, and it takes a king's wisdom to stay balanced on such a thoroughbred steed.

As Christians fast, the world consumes the Church (in the same way that we "eat Jesus"). But when victory comes, as it always, inevitably does, we feast. Then the kings of the earth bring in their glory: the Church consumes the world. This is how it will be, to and fro, until both Church and state are transfigured figures.

---

2   "The world is like a drunken peasant. If you lift him into the saddle on one side, he will fall off again on the other side." – Martin Luther, *Table Talk*.

And so much the more...

"Whenever the devil
pesters you, at once seek
out the company of
friends, drink more,
joke and jest, or engage
in some form of
merriment."

— Martin Luther

Recommended Reading

James B. Jordan

Through New Eyes, Developing A Biblical View Of The World

From Bread To Wine: Toward A More Biblical Liturgical Theology

Studies In Food And Faith

Peter J. Leithart

Blessed Are The Hungry: Meditations On The Lord's Supper

Against Christianity

Douglas Jones and Douglas Wilson

Angels In The Architecture: A Protestant Vision For Middle Earth

---

Steve Wilkins

Face To Face: Meditations On Friendship And Hospitality

Robert Farrar Capon

The Supper Of The Lamb: A Culinary Reflection

90228033R00212

Made in the USA
Columbia, SC
28 February 2018